Technology-Enhanced Teaching and Learning

Leading and Supporting the Transformation on Your Campus

EDUCAUSE
Leadership Strategies No. 5

JOSSEY-BASS
A Wiley Company
San Francisco

Published by

JOSSEY-BASS
A Wiley Company
350 Sansome St.
San Francisco, CA 94104

www.josseybass.com

Copyright © 2001 by John Wiley & Sons, Inc.

Jossey-Bass is a registered trademark of John Wiley & Sons, Inc.

This book is part of the Jossey-Bass Higher and Adult Education Series.

Jossey-Bass books and products are available through most bookstores. To contact Jossey-Bass directly, call (888) 378-2537, fax to (800) 605-2665, or visit our website at www.josseybass.com.

Substantial discounts on bulk quantities of Jossey-Bass books are available to corporations, professional associations, and other organizations. For details and discount information, contact the special sales department at Jossey-Bass.

We at Jossey-Bass strive to use the most environmentally sensitive paper stocks available to us. Our publications are printed on acid-free recycled stock whenever possible, and our paper always meets or exceeds minimum GPO and EPA requirements.

Library of Congress Cataloging-in-Publication Data

Technology-enhanced teaching and learning: leading and supporting the transformation on your campus / Carole A. Barone, Paul R. Hagner, editors.
     p. cm.—(EDUCAUSE leadership strategies; no. 5)
Includes bibliographical references and index.
    ISBN 0-7879-5013-0 (pbk.: alk. paper)
    1. Education, Higher—Effect of technological innovations on—United States.
2. Universities and colleges—United States—Data processing.   I. Barone, Carole A., date– II. Hagner, Paul R.   III. Series.
    LB2395.7.T43   2001
    378'.00285—dc21   2001003161

FIRST EDITION
PB Printing   10 9 8 7 6 5 4 3 2 1

Technology-Enhanced Teaching and Learning

Carole A. Barone,
Paul R. Hagner, Editors

The EDUCAUSE Leadership Strategies series addresses critical themes related to information technology that will shape higher education in the years to come. The series is intended to make a significant contribution to the knowledge academic leaders can draw upon to chart a course for their institutions into a technology-based future. Books in the series offer practical advice and guidelines to help campus leaders develop action plans to further that end. The series is developed by EDUCAUSE and published by Jossey-Bass. The sponsorship of PricewaterhouseCoopers LLP makes it possible for EDUCAUSE to distribute complimentary copies of books in the series to more than 1,800 EDUCAUSE member institutions, organizations, and corporations.

EDUCAUSE

EDUCAUSE is an international nonprofit association with offices in Boulder, Colorado, and Washington, D.C. The association is dedicated to helping shape and enable transformational change in higher education through the introduction, use, and management of information resources and technologies in teaching, learning, scholarship, research, and institutional management. EDUCAUSE activities include an educational program of conferences, workshops, seminars, and institutes; a variety of print and on-line publications; strategic/policy initiatives such as the National Learning Infrastructure Initiative, the Net@EDU program, and the Center for Applied Research; and extensive Web-based information services.

EDUCAUSE
- provides professional development opportunities for those involved with planning for, managing, and using information technologies in colleges and universities
- seeks to influence policy by working with leaders in the education, corporate, and government sectors who have a stake in the transformation of higher education through information technologies
- enables the transfer of leading-edge approaches to information technology management and use that are developed and shared through EDUCAUSE policy and strategy initiatives
- provides a forum for dialogue between information resources professionals and campus leaders at all levels
- keeps members informed about information technology innovations, strategies, and practices that may affect their campuses, identifying and researching the most pressing issues

Current EDUCAUSE membership includes more than 1,800 campuses, organizations, and corporations. For up-to-date information about EDUCAUSE programs, initiatives, and services, visit the association's Web site at www.educause.edu, send e-mail to info@educause.edu, or call 303-449-4430.

PRICEWATERHOUSE COOPERS

PricewaterhouseCoopers is a leading provider of professional services to institutions of higher education, serving a full range of educational institutions—from small colleges to large public and private universities to educational companies.

PricewaterhouseCoopers (www.pwcglobal.com) is the world's largest professional services organization, drawing on the knowledge and skills of more than 150,000 people in 150 countries to help clients solve complex business problems and measurably enhance their ability to build value, manage risk, and improve performance in an Internet-enabled world.

PricewaterhouseCoopers refers to the member firms of the worldwide PricewaterhouseCoopers organization.

Contents

Foreword

There have been few moments in human experience where we can say with a great sense of certainty that our world is about to change in a dramatic and revolutionary way. For all of us who are partici-pants in the world of higher education, such a moment is at hand.

In writing about the nature of scientific revolutions, Thomas Kuhn (1970) likened the revolutionary period to one in which "it is as if the professional community had been suddenly transported to another planet where familiar objects are seen in a different light and are joined by unfamiliar ones as well" (p. 111). In a very real sense, a similar form of transport is confronting those of us in higher education leadership right now. Dramatic advances in information technology are forcing us to reexamine all of the familiar objects that occupy our academic landscape while presenting a daunting as-sortment of new and unfamiliar technologies and applications that must be incorporated as well. This incorporation goes well beyond augmenting what we do already; it changes the very nature of what we do. This change manifests itself all the way down to the level of the basic concepts and definitions we have comfortably lived with all of our professional lives. Words such as *student, teacher, teaching, learning, campus,* and *semester* have all had their denotations and connotations changed or expanded by the capabilities and capaci-ties provided by the new technologies. Kuhn also suggested that "at times of revolution . . . the scientist's perception of the environment must be re-educated—in some familiar situations [he or she] must learn to see a new gestalt" (p. 112).

Technology-Enhanced Teaching and Learning: Leading and Supporting the Transformation on Your Campus is not designed to produce this new gestalt; rather, the chapters proceed on the assumption that because the impact of the new technologies is pervasive, the response of the institution must be systemic and engage all relevant services and functions. Once you and your colleagues have begun to make this shift, you will find the discussions that follow to be useful in facing the substantial task of guiding your institution into the new, information-rich environment. In a sense, what follows is a guidebook for a new reality where the familiar is transformed and the unfamiliar is incorporated.

JOHN C. HITT
President
University of Central Florida

Reference

Kuhn, T. S. *The Structure of Scientific Revolutions*. (2nd ed.) Chicago: University of Chicago Press, 1970.

Preface

Because it is our human ingenuity that creates technological change, we harbor the belief that we are in control of these technologies and their impacts on society. History shows, however, that technological advances often move much faster than our own cultural abilities to shape them.

The twentieth century has provided numerous examples of this phenomenon. Commercial radio broadcasts started in 1920, but it took the federal government almost a decade to understand the potential societal impact of nationwide information sharing and to begin to regulate the new technology. The nuclear bomb produced the politics and policies of the cold war. The impact of television on interpersonal interactions, values, and behaviors has been well documented. Most recently, the revolutionary advances in genetics research will force significant rethinking of medical practices, policies, ethics, and indeed human history (Wade, 2000).

Similarly, computing and communication technologies have made it possible to send and receive massive amounts of information, voice, and even video signals rapidly through the Internet and the World Wide Web. These new capabilities, together with the development of huge stores of on-line information of all types that can be accessed at any time through this network, are changing the basic structures and operations of organizations, especially educational institutions.

For each technological advance, there is a social and political reactive adjustment. The anticipation and speed of this adjustment depend heavily on the level of knowledge and preparation of key decision makers.

Higher education, as a societal entity, is not immune to this process. However, higher education is a fairly traditional marketplace and so far has made relatively few adaptations in the way it conducts business in this powerful new networked communications environment. History informs us that this resistance cannot, and will not, persist (Hawkins, 2000).

Transformative Change and Leadership

This book is about higher education leadership and transformation in the information age. By *transformation*, we mean radical change in the function and form of the teaching and learning environment, which, at least for some institutions, will lead to a change in identity and market. What specifically is being transformed within this environment? Everything and more!

These transformations are ranging from augmentation of the traditional forms of teaching and learning and communicating with students to the establishment of an on-line presence that emphasizes virtual learning. We added "and more" because it is not just teaching and learning that are affected in the transformation process. In the new environments, every service delivery function of the institution is integrated with the process of teaching and learning. New advances in technology allow us to rethink every aspect of how a college or university runs. In a very real sense, the most important first step in this transformation process occurs within our heads: we must first transform ourselves.

Transformation means disruptive change, and society as a result is changing faster than anyone's ability to control it. This book provides actionable advice for leaders who are motivated to strive for a graceful transition to a set of institutional values and conventions appropriate to the information age. It is not necessarily easy reading, intellectually or emotionally. However, we believe that the book's message will capture the interest of leaders with the courage to risk a change in perspective and perhaps lead them to engage differently in their institutional decision-making processes.

The fact that you are reading this book indicates that although you may not necessarily endorse the change that is coming, you acknowledge its arrival. This arrival will not come in the form of a revolutionary wave that sweeps all nontransformed institutions away in its wake. As Robert Wallhaus (2000) notes, "Traditional models will still exist, so new technologies will have to be compatible with traditional measures of the learning experience" (p. 21). However, it is important to note that this process of evolutionary adaptation will be propelled at higher speeds as the technology rapidly shifts and as the more responsive and adaptive elements in the external environment—most notably the private sector—react and adapt more swiftly than higher education to the emerging communications technologies. Not today, not tomorrow, but in the very near future, higher education administrators will have to face the reverse of Wallhaus's challenge: accommodate traditional models of learning deliveries within the new environment created by technological teaching and learning innovations.

Students Are Already Transformed

An additional impetus to this fast-track evolutionary transformation process is that technology has already had a major impact on the central targets of teaching and learning: students. The fact that students are already arriving with a familiarity with the new technologies is an important, but obvious, point. What is more essential to the topic of institutional readiness for transformation is that the students are coming with an established experience in distributed learning. They are now accustomed to being able to access information anytime, anywhere; to constructing personal repositories of knowledge from fragments of information gathered on the Web; and to interacting with and learning from others in virtual environments (Frand, 2000).

Television made students of the 1980s and 1990s more oriented to the visual than the textual. In a similar fashion, the students of the new millennium will be accustomed to, *and will demand,* interactive learning technologies that will less and less resemble the traditional delivery systems that currently exist in most higher education institutions. As Alan Kay, one of the creators of the Apple Macintosh, noted in a lecture at the University of California–Los Angeles in 1996, technology is "anything that isn't around when you were born." To today's and tomorrow's students, computers and all their assorted add-ons are not technologies; they are expectations.

An Institutional Challenge

An institution's faculty and administration will confront the new demands and expectations. Transformation is not just a faculty challenge; it is an institutional challenge (Oblinger, Barone, and Hawkins, 2001). This important observation is the source of the dynamic tension that exists on campuses today. Campus leaders can no longer evade the challenge of institutional commitment. It is not simply the case of putting new instructional tools in the hands of faculty, but rather creating an institutional environment that uses the new tools and philosophies of learning delivery in a way that is compatible with how faculty now must operate.

The institution is responsible for providing the support and nourishment necessary to allow faculty to adapt and transform—a primary condition for institutional transformation. Over time, new faculty roles and behaviors will evolve from the institution's point of commitment to transformation. The chapters in this book focus on elements that are key to initiating that transformation at the core of the institution and to sustaining and supporting it once it has begun.

Individual institutional transformation efforts are not occurring in a vacuum. Early in 2001, the President's Information Technology Committee (PITAC) issued a report containing findings and recommendations based on a year-long study of the use and importance of the emerging technologies to traditional education and to lifelong learning. The overarching finding of the PITAC report was that "education and training of all citizens throughout their lives is one of our most important national goals. Information technology promises to play a significant role in empowering teachers and learners" (p. 4). The report recommended that the integration of information technology with education and training be a national priority. Thus, the transformation that your campus is either contemplating or undergoing can be viewed as part of a broader higher education agenda; it is the direction that every institution will eventually need to take.

This book, then, is predicated on the assumption of the inevitability and acceptance of this transformation. It also assumes that this transformative change cannot occur in one or two isolated corners of the institution but must represent a systematic response across the broad, interrelated spectrum that makes up the institution, its environment, and its clientele.

What This Book Offers

We assume that this book's readers are leaders who are committed to institutional transformation and are willing to make the requisite personal and institutional choices. The chapter authors offer insights into faculty attitudes, behaviors, and values, as well as practical suggestions for strategic actions that might be taken to engage the campus community in the transformation process. They probe the decision-making process and offer new insights into appropriate leadership behavior in this emerging institutional environment.

We begin with the chapter by Paul R. Hagner and Charles A. Schneebeck on faculty engagement to emphasize our belief that what happens in the faculty-student dyad lies at the core of an institution's mission. All other institutional services and structures, many of them discussed in subsequent chapters, are established to nurture this core relationship. Hagner and Schneebeck describe different types of faculty motivations for embracing and resisting transformation and suggest strategies for engagement based on these motivations.

In Chapter Two, David G. Brown and Sally Jackson examine change at the institutional level, discussing opposing presumptions concerning change and offering practical measures that institutional leaders can take to manage the resulting tensions to energize the decision-making environment.

Following the different perspectives on change presented in the first two chapters, Chapter Three addresses the way that institutions can deal with the inevitable complexity that transformation produces. Vicki N. Suter offers an alternative way of thinking about institutional governance that she argues is more appropriate to the values and culture of the transformed institution.

In Chapter Four, William H. Graves takes us beyond the question of faculty engagement presented in Chapter One and clarifies the role of faculty members in the new learning environment. While explicating how technology increases the options for learning, Graves acknowledges and honors the role of faculty members in the development and use of learningware, which he suggests is the logical extension of the traditional textbook in a technology-enhanced learning environment. He wisely argues that the time has come for faculty to participate in informed debate about effective practices in virtual education.

In Chapter Five, Joel L. Hartman and Barbara Truman-Davis discuss more explicitly how to make this change possible. They explore the systemic changes necessary to provide a sustainable and scalable faculty support structure and emphasize that team-based support efforts offer the best possibilities for nurturing transformations.

The team concept is elaborated on in Chapter Six by Gerard L. Hanley, who offers a framework for both designing new and using existing instructional technology to enhance student learning, using the experience of The California State University's Center for Distributed Learning to illustrate the success of the framework.

Policy, like physical infrastructure, is part of the framework for transition. Intellectual property policy, at both the national and the institutional levels, lags faculty practice and often serves to inhibit necessary adaptations in the teaching and learning environment. In Chapter Seven, James L. Hilton and James G. Neal provide an overview of the shifting intellectual property environment. They argue that the social obligation of higher education requires involvement beyond the traditional residential campus. To meet that obligation and remain viable in an increasingly competitive market, institutions must address the policy and legal underpinnings of the educational enterprise.

With regard to the infrastructure needed to support the transformation, it is important for leaders to know what kinds of questions to ask, to ask those questions, and to have some high-level sense of what the answers mean. In Chapter Eight, Bret L. Ingerman raises a series of strategic questions that explore issues of infrastructure as they relate to overall institutional strategy. He suggests the kinds of questions that presidents and provosts should ask to link infrastructure to institutional goals and helps leaders to interpret the answers to those questions in the context of institutional culture, policy, and goals. Presidents and boards of trustees or regents need to understand that in times of transition, participation in infrastructure decisions—because they relate to institutional goals and character—is an obligation of executive oversight.

Finally, in the closing chapter, we present a framework of twelve conditions for campus transformation that manifest themselves throughout the eight previous chapters.

This book is neither a theoretic discourse on change nor a how-to manual. Its purpose is to heighten readers' awareness of how progressive institutions are initiating, implementing, and ultimately managing transformation in the new Web-based communication and learning environments. These changes are inevitable. We hope that this book will convey important information and warning signs to help you on your path to transformation.

June 2001   PAUL R. HAGNER
                                                     CAROLE A. BARONE

References

Frand, J. L. "The Information-Age Mindset: Changes in Students and Implications for Higher Education." *EDUCAUSE Review*, Sept.–Oct. 2000, pp. 15–24.

Hawkins, B. L. "Technology, Education, and a Very Foggy Crystal Ball." *EDUCAUSE Review*, Nov.–Dec. 2000, pp. 65–73.

Oblinger, D. G., Barone, C. A., and Hawkins, B. L. *Distributed Education and Its Challenges: An Overview*. Washington, D.C.: American Council on Education and EDUCAUSE, 2001.

President's Information Technology Advisory Committee. *Using Technology to Transform the Way We Learn*. Washington, D.C.: President's Information Technology Advisory Committee, 2001. [www.ccic.gov/pubs/pitac/pitac-tl-9feb01.pdf].

Wade, N. "Scientists Rough Out Humanity's 50,000-Year-Old Story." *New York Times Online*, Nov. 14, 2000.

Wallhaus, R. A. "E-Learning: From Institutions to Providers, from Students to Learners." In R. Katz and D. Oblinger (eds.), *The "E" Is for Everything: E-Commerce, E-Business, and E-Learning in Higher Education*. San Francisco: Jossey-Bass, 2000.

Acknowledgments

Although our names appear as editors on the title page, this book has been a truly collaborative effort of all those who contributed to its development.

We would first like to thank the authors who contributed their "learned lessons" to the chapters, for their creativity in adjusting to the theme of the book and their patience as we integrated the chapters and focused our collective message. To be honest, we drew up our list of possible contributors with a bit of trepidation. The experience, insight, and expertise that put each name on the list also meant that each of these individuals would already have a full professional plate and our invitation to contribute a chapter might represent an overflow. This was, in fact, the case, but each author was willing to accommodate our request in spite of his or her busy schedule. For this we are profoundly grateful.

We would also like to thank both our personal and professional families. Our families at home tolerated, with good will, late night e-mailing and phone calling, especially in the later stages of the book's development. Our professional families provided us with fresh insights and encouragement to persist in our advocacy of higher education transformation. We would especially like to thank the professional family that we both shared last year, the staff of the National Learning Infrastructure Initiative: Vicki Suter, Tor Cross, and Anne Archambault.

Readers of other volumes in the EDUCAUSE Leadership Strate-gies series have seen the name Julia A. Rudy featured prominently in each acknowledgments section, and with good reason. Julie's hand and influence can be seen throughout our book. She func-tioned far less as a series editor and far more as a collaborator, con-science, and well-informed taskmaster for the project. It is too easy to state that the quality of this book would have suffered greatly if she had not been involved; a more accurate statement would be that this book would not have happened at all without her wise and informed guidance.

We would also like to thank PricewaterhouseCoopers for gen-erous support of the EDUCAUSE Leadership Strategies series, which ensures the distribution of each volume to more than 1,800 EDUCAUSE representatives at member campuses, organizations, and corporations.

Finally, the editors would like to thank each other for the colle-giality and good humor that has marked our working relationship. We began the project as colleagues and ended as good friends.

C.A.B.
P.R.H.

The Authors

Carole A. Barone is vice president of EDUCAUSE, where her responsibilities include a focus on the National Learning Infrastructure Initiative and teaching and learning programs. Previously, she was associate vice chancellor for information technology at the University of California at Davis and vice president for information systems and computing at Syracuse University. Barone serves on the boards of IMS Global Learning Consortium, Inc., and New Media Centers and is a member of the advisory board of the Multimedia Educational Resource for Learning and Online Teaching (MERLOT) project. She was the 1995 recipient of the CAUSE ELITE Award for Exemplary Leadership and Information Technology Excellence. She holds master's and doctoral degrees from the Maxwell School of Citizenship and Public Affairs at Syracuse University.

Paul R. Hagner is a special adviser for technology planning and assessment at the University of Hartford. Previously he spent eighteen years on the faculty at Washington State University, where he served as chair of the political science department and received the university's William F. Mullen Award for Teaching Excellence, and five years on the faculty at The University of Memphis, where he was also departmental chair. Hagner has made many professional presentations and authored numerous articles and a book on the subject of political behavior. In 2000, he served as a fellow for EDU-CAUSE's National Learning Infrastructure Initiative, focusing on the area of technological transformation of higher education institutions. Hagner received his Ph.D. in political science from Indiana University.

David G. Brown, formerly provost and now a vice president at Wake Forest University, is professor of economics and dean of the International Center for Computer Enhanced Learning. He previously served as president of Transylvania University and chancellor of the University of North Carolina at Asheville. He founded the Annual Conference of Ubiquitous Computing for Colleges and Universities and the Gallery of Courses Taught with Technology; has authored and edited half a dozen books and dozens of articles on electronically enhanced education; publishes a monthly column in *Syllabus*; and serves on the editorial board of *Multiversity*. An active user of technology in his own classroom, Brown was recognized as an "inspirational teacher of undergraduates" by the University of North Carolina at Chapel Hill.

William H. Graves is chairman and founder of Eduprise, a higher education information technology service company. Previously, he was professor and chief information officer at the University of North Carolina at Chapel Hill and was founder and director of the Institute for Academic Technology. Graves has given hundreds of presentations, published more than fifty articles, and served as a higher education consultant on educational uses of technology. He is a member of the boards of COLLEGIS, EDUCAUSE, and the IMS Global Learning Consortium; chairs the National Learning Infrastructure Initiative Planning Committee; and serves on the applications strategy council of the University Corporation for Advanced Internet Development and its Internet2 project. He earned his Ph.D. in mathematics at Indiana University.

Gerard L. Hanley is senior director of Academic Technology Services at The California State University (CSU) Office of the Chancellor and program manager for the Multimedia Educational Resource for Learning and Online Teaching (MERLOT) project. He oversees the development and implementation of integrated electronic library resources and academic technology to support the instructional and research programs of the CSU system's twenty-three campuses. Previously, Hanley held the positions of director of faculty development and director of strategic planning at the CSU Long Beach campus. He received his B.A., M.A., and Ph.D. degrees in psychology from the State University of New York at Stony Brook.

Joel L. Hartman is vice provost for information technologies and resources at the University of Central Florida, with overall responsibility for the library, computing, networking, telecommunications, media services, and distributed-learning technology activities. Previously, he was chief information officer at Bradley University. Hartman has been an information technology consultant to both public and private sector organizations and has been active in the development of state educational telecommunications policy and resources in Illinois and Florida. He serves on the EDUCAUSE board of directors and the National Learning Infrastructure Initiative Planning Committee. Hartman received his bachelor's and master's degrees in journalism and communication from the University of Illinois, Urbana-Champaign, and is completing doctoral work at the University of Central Florida.

James L. Hilton is professor of psychology at the University of Michigan. As associate provost for academic, information, and instructional technology affairs, he is responsible for examining the implications that new media and technology raise for higher education and for developing and implementing policies that respond to the particular needs that confront large, complex research universities. His scholarly interests focus on stereotypes, the psychology of suspicion, and multimedia pedagogy. Hilton is a three-time recipient of the College of Literature, Science and the Arts Excellence in Education Award, has been named an Arthur F. Thurnau Professor (1997–2000), and received the Class of 1923 Memorial Teaching Award. Hilton received his Ph.D. in psychology from Princeton University.

Bret L. Ingerman is chief technology officer and director of the Center for Information Technology Services at Skidmore College. He is responsible for strategic planning and operations of all information technology functions at the college, including user support, server and network management, telecommunications, administrative databases, computer purchase recommendations, and logistics, technical support, and media services. Previously, he was assistant vice president for information technology at Lewis & Clark College and served in a number of computing and instructional positions at Syracuse University, where he earned his B.S. and M.S. degrees in psychology. He has also held adjunct teaching positions, instructing both faculty and students in the use of instructional technologies.

Sally Jackson is professor of communication and vice provost for faculty development and educational technology at the University of Arizona. Previously, she served on the communication faculties of the University of Nebraska–Lincoln, Michigan State University, and Oklahoma University. Jackson's main research interest is argumentation, for which she has received numerous awards. Her closely related work in communication research methods has also received scholarly awards, most notably the National Communication Association's Charles H. Woolbert Award for social science research of lasting and demonstrable impact. Her academic background is in speech communication, in which she received bachelor's and master's degrees, as well as the Ph.D., from the University of Illinois at Urbana-Champaign.

James G. Neal is dean of University Libraries and Sheridan Director of the Milton S. Eisenhower Library at Johns Hopkins University. Previously, he was dean of University Libraries at Indiana University and held administrative positions in the libraries at Penn State, Notre Dame, and the City University of New York. At Johns Hopkins, he also oversees the Center for Educational Resources, the Digital Knowledge Center, and the Library Entrepreneurial Program. Neal is active on the national and international levels in the areas of copyright policy and legislation and scholarly communication and publishing. He has served on the executive board of the American Library Association and was president of the Association of Research Libraries. He received an M.A. in history and M.S. and advanced certificate in library science from Columbia University.

Charles A. Schneebeck recently retired from the Office of the Chancellor of The California State University (CSU), where he was director of the CSU Center for Distributed Learning. The center's purpose is to explore new technologies for learning, with a focus on identifying learning problems and applying technology in support of appropriate pedagogy. Schneebeck is the founder of the Multimedia Educational Resource for Learning and Online Teaching (MERLOT) project, which provides tools that allow faculty to share teaching and learning resources over the World Wide Web. He also produced the Web-based Biology Labs Online series that is being marketed by Addison-Wesley Longman Publishing Company. Previously he held the position of director of academic computing services, first at Fullerton College and then at Long Beach State University.

Vicki N. Suter is director of projects for EDUCAUSE's National Learning Infrastructure Initiative. She has over twenty years of experience in coordinating technical projects and programs, developing information technology strategic plans for a wide range of organizations, and conducting research on telecommuting, community networking, and distance education. She was a founder of the successful Davis Community Network and contributor to the literature on "smart communities," those that build an advanced telecommunications infrastructure to remain economically competitive in the new global economy while ensuring that the technology transforms the entire community in positive ways. Suter received an M.B.A. from the University of California, Davis, and holds an undergraduate degree in economics.

Barbara Truman-Davis is director of Course Development and Web Services (CD&WS) at the University of Central Florida. CD&WS supports the university's on-line degrees and programs and has responsibility for faculty, staff, and course development. The unit is also responsible for campuswide Web activities, including the university's main Web site. CD&WS teams are made up of instructional designers, digital media specialists, Web developers, Web analysts, video services specialists, and software engineers who collaborate to produce multimedia and Web-based resources. Truman-Davis is active in statewide committees for faculty development and student services. Her research interests include computer-supported collaborative learning and virtual teams. She holds a master's degree in instructional systems design from the University of Central Florida and is completing doctoral studies in curriculum and instruction, specializing in Web-based learning.

Technology-Enhanced
Teaching and Learning

1

Engaging the Faculty

Paul R. Hagner, Charles A. Schneebeck

The faculty-student dyad lies at the heart of the teaching and learning process. The revolution in communication technologies has opened the door to a wide variety of teaching and learning materials that can lead to new teaching and learning environments that have not been possible in the past. The challenge for today's college or university is how to change its environment to accommodate and promote the use of these new technologies better.

Perhaps the most critical component in institutional transformation of teaching and learning through new technologies is faculty engagement. In this chapter, we address how to encourage, engage, and nurture faculty as they set about to alter fundamentally one of the most important aspects of their professional lives. We explore several characteristics associated with faculty values and orientations toward the adoption of the new teaching technologies, and we illustrate how an external, Web-based resource can serve the needs of different types of faculty during the transformation process.

The Challenge of Faculty Autonomy

Faculty come to their profession as the result of a variety of motivational structures, and they vary tremendously in the way they perform their assigned tasks (Blackburn, 1995). This variation is sustained by the fact that as they progress up the tenure and promotion ladder, it

1

becomes increasingly difficult for administration to influence almost any aspect of their job performance.

As Steven M. Cahn (1986) observed, "Few institutions other than colleges and universities permit their members the latitude so much a part of the professor's life" (p. 3). The tradition-bound nature of the academy has accommodated this latitude, and the slow pace of change in almost every aspect of campus life has made it a tolerable part of the academic landscape. However, the complacency and comfort of that landscape is now shifting.

Technological change has removed the spatial security of academic institutions by opening up and redefining the core concept of the delivery of learning. This fact, coupled with the change in the nature and expectations of students, has produced a strong impetus for change and transformation. In a real sense, faculty will feel the pressure from both above and below: from administrators reacting to market forces and from students who demand new forms of learning presentation. In the face of growing pressure to adapt to these new circumstances, faculty autonomy presents a considerable challenge.

How Faculty View the New Technologies

The theory of Everett Rogers (1995) on the diffusion of innovation has quite deservedly been recognized as the baseline work in this area. We offer a simplified version of Rogers's adopter classification categories that we believe can be useful in understanding faculty on the basis of their underlying motivational states with regard to using emerging technologies to change the way they teach.

Certainly, the complexity of faculty roles makes such a classification far too simplistic for many purposes, as many faculty possess characteristics of more than one of the four groups we describe. However, after intensive interviews with over 240 faculty at the University of Hartford, we have found that they demonstrate predominant characteristics of one of the four groups and that these characteristics appear to be related to the probability that the faculty member will or will not adopt new ways of teaching and learning.

The First Wave: The Entrepreneurs

Sometimes referred to as "lone rangers" (Bates, 2000), these professors represent the vanguard of innovation and risk taking in teaching and learning. David G. Brown (2000) edited a highly informative book that collected ninety-three vignettes describing the work done by entrepreneurial professors. As a follow-up, Paul R. Hagner (2000) interviewed roughly half of these entrepreneurs to explore their motivations for their novel work. These interviews revealed both a high level of commitment to quality teaching and learning and an informed competency with the new teaching and learning technologies.

Although entrepreneurs do not seek rewards or recognition for their work, they nevertheless are rather disappointed when there is an absence of positive feedback. One other important characteristic of their work is that it tends to be idiosyncratic and not portable to other faculty. Basically, entrepreneurial faculty are content to use their expertise to solve their own instructional problems.

The Second Wave: The Risk Aversives

This second group of faculty is perhaps the most interesting. Although they share the commitment of the first-wave faculty to quality learning, they are more risk aversive (Geoghegan, 1998). They can have one or more of the following characteristics:

- Lacking technical expertise, they are unsure of the investment costs associated with transformation.
- They are afraid that their current success in teaching will not translate into the new teaching environments.
- They will need significant levels of instructional support to make the transformation.
- They are hesitant to become engaged in the process of self-examination (in terms of developing learning

objectives) that is demanded by the new forms of learning delivery.

It is important to keep in mind that these faculty members are committed to quality teaching and learning and that they are attracted to the new technologies because of the potential for improving what they do. A critical first step is to provide information to faculty in this group that can demonstrate the effectiveness of the new forms of teaching, including examples of success stories from faculty they consider peers. The second step is to create a support environment that facilitates their transition. Adoption of technology for teaching and learning by second-wave faculty is inversely proportional to the effort they must exert. They want to focus on teaching and learning, not on the technology.

The Third Wave: The Reward Seekers

As colleges and universities change their reward structures in the tenure and promotion process, a third wave of faculty will emerge: those who see adopting technology-based teaching techniques as a way to advance their professional careers. These faculty members' motivational structure is tied closely to the university's reward structure. When they view adoption of new teaching and learning techniques as having a positive impact on tenure, promotion, and salary decisions, they will be more willing to transform.

Colleges and universities should be willing to adjust the reward and recognition structure so that it is aligned with new institutional priorities. As long as this structure attempts to strike a balance between the old and the new, there will be less incentive to adapt to the new environment.

The Reluctants

The fourth group of faculty members includes those who are computer illiterate or firmly believe that traditional models of learning are superior. For this reason, we do not consider this group to constitute a wave. Although numerous examples across the nation have shown that it is neither time- nor cost-effective to attempt to incorporate philosophically resistant faculty into institutional transformation, there is a very important human factor to consider when dealing with these individuals.

With the incorporation of the computer into university research in the 1970s, many faculty, especially those in the social sciences, found that the type of research they had done in the past to establish their professional careers was no longer acceptable to the professional journals. The shifting of emphasis from teaching to research during this period exacerbated their difficulties. Universities at that time offered little in support of these mostly older faculty, and as a result, many sought early retirement or ended their careers on bitter notes. There is a high probability that we shall see a similar process emerge around the issue of the adoption of new learning technologies.

As their colleagues either bring in or adopt the new technologies and as students come to expect and respond positively to them, the reluctants may well be confronted with a contrast effect that may have an adverse impact on the evaluation of their teaching. While they have not changed the way they teach, the world around them will have changed. They will find themselves to be increasingly anachronistic.

Although the decision not to adopt new forms of presentation is the choice of the faculty member, it is nonetheless important to alert faculty to the personal consequences of this decision. In our work in this area at our institutions, we have found it very effective to have this message communicated by a faculty member to other faculty members and faculty bodies, such as faculty senates. The more information concerning the effectiveness of the new technologies in the teaching and learning process that can be provided to these faculty, the better. Rejection of better ways to perform their jobs makes their nonparticipation an overt act rather than one of benign avoidance. Overall, these approaches make transformation more of a faculty-student concern than an administrative concern.

First Step: Know Your Faculty

Before your institution can begin the transformation process, you must first be able to determine what mix of faculty groups you have. The choice of engagement strategy depends on this important element of institutional readiness information. For instance, many universities have made the mistake of setting up their support structures on the basis of the characteristics of the entrepreneurs. This "if you build it, they will come" mentality has created consternation for administrators, because their costly investment in hardware and infrastructure overlooked the fact that many faculty, especially the risk aversives, needed flesh-and-blood support to make their transformation. In these instances, many well-equipped support centers see few new faces.

Institutions need to determine their faculty mix. Transformations in colleges and universities dominated by either the first or last group of faculty members are easy to predict; they occur quickly in the first case and emerge only after a long period of attrition and replacement in the last. Institutions dominated by faculty in either of the middle groups will have to make a commitment to providing significant faculty support even if the infrastructure is in place. Obviously, if the risk aversives dominate, then emphasis on infrastructure and strong support will create a much better chance for successful transformation. The domination of the third group of faculty makes this effort more problematic because it involves a restructuring and redefinition of the institutional reward structure prior to adoption. This slows the transformation process considerably because most administrators are reluctant to engage in the politics of their institution's reward structure without a clear assurance of tangible gain as a result of that engagement.

In preparing an inventory of faculty proclivities, some institutions are designating individuals to make contact with all faculty members to assess their current use of technology and their possible future use. This is a time-intensive process that works well only in smaller institutions. Some institutions are using e-mail surveys to all faculty. This method is also not usually very effective because response rates for faculty surveys are notoriously low and this method misses faculty who do not use e-mail on a regular basis, causing a bias in the results. We have found the most success in our efforts from using the department chair as the reporting source. Most chairs have a good sense of their faculty's computer expertise.

The most important element of this information-gathering process, regardless of means chosen, is to make it public. A common concern on the part of faculty is that central administration rarely makes the effort to solicit faculty input. An intensive and very open effort to gather faculty-based information pays off well when the time comes for making specific policy. If policymaking is tied at least in part to the information collected from faculty, a greater sense of legitimacy and a greater probability of cooperation are obtained.

Roughly the same process can be used to gather input from students. Since students will be the direct recipients of the changes brought about by transformation, their participation in and approval of the use of new technologies are important. Many institutions are sponsoring open forums with students, in established or ad hoc groupings, to discuss issues relating to transformation. Those who have run these sessions report high levels of student interest and enthusiasm. Communicating these student reactions to the faculty can also provide useful arguments for engagement.

An External Source of Faculty Engagement

Can faculty with varying motivational states for adopting technologies be served by the use of innovative resources that are available to all institutions? We believe that one such resource, the Multimedia Educational Resource for Learning and Online Teaching (MERLOT) project, can be used effectively by a wide variety of faculty who come to the technology table for different reasons.

Although the number of faculty who want to use the power of computers and networks is increasing, finding a sufficient quantity of high-quality interactive teaching and learning materials remains difficult. The MERLOT project (www.merlot.org) is addressing this barrier to the effective use of these technologies by providing tools that allow faculty to share teaching and learning resources over the World Wide Web. Thousands of faculty from across the country are collaborating to create a collection of on-line teaching and learning materials that can be shared by the entire higher education community. This approach is being sponsored by the National Learning Infrastructure Initiative (NLII) of EDUCAUSE and twenty-three institutional partnerships throughout North America.

MERLOT recognizes the fact that each year more faculty want to incorporate technology into their teaching and learning environments, yet only a small percentage of faculty actually develop Web-based, interactive learning material. Because the publishing industry is not meeting the growing need for these materials, MERLOT is providing an environment where higher education can collaborate to address this critical need.

Members of the MERLOT community add value to the collection of teaching and learning materials in a number of ways. For example, they use the MERLOT tools to add assignments to individual learning materials, an activity that provides examples of appropriate pedagogy for other members of the community. Perhaps the most significant value added by the community of users is a peer review process to ensure quality control. Similar to the scholarly peer review process, the MERLOT peer review process provides a mechanism for faculty who create Web-based, interactive learning materials to have their work evaluated by their peers from other institutions. A less formal mechanism for quality control is the ability of any member of the MERLOT community to add user comments about any of the learning materials found in the collection.

MERLOT can be a powerful engagement tool because its features can appeal to faculty at all stages of engagement.

Entrepreneurs

Of course, by definition the entrepreneurs are already engaged, but that engagement tends to be personal rather than collaborative. MERLOT offers two incentives for entrepreneurial faculty members to broaden the reach of their work. First, it offers the opportunity for them to display what they have done to a wider audience. This is a form of engagement since it gives the entrepreneurs the opportunity to see that their work can be leveraged beyond the needs of their classroom. Second, MERLOT gives the entrepreneurs a chance to interact with other entrepreneurs in their field of expertise. Smaller institutions may have very few entrepreneurs, and they are working in considerable isolation with little entrepreneur-to-entrepreneur interaction. MERLOT allows the entrepreneurial faculty member to become a part of a wider virtual community.

Risk Aversives

The most defining aspect of members of this faculty group is that the easier the institution makes their transition, the better their chance of transformation will be. While this can usually translate into improvements in the faculty support area (see Chapter Five), many institutions lack the resources to offer course content development services to all interested faculty. MERLOT offers faculty not only the learning packages themselves, but also peer-based guidance on how to apply them in classes. The main goal of the project is to eliminate the traditional barriers associated with the incorporation of new technologies, chief of which is the faculty member's reluctance to assume a student role once again.

Reward Seekers

The impact of the new technologies goes far beyond the teacher-learner dyad. Transformations in teaching and learning are now being accompanied by transformations in the very meaning of research and scholarship. At each level of the hierarchy at a university (departmental, college, and central), there will need to be a redefinition process that will incorporate the new forms of virtual scholarship. This is especially important because the faculty most likely to possess the expertise, or at least possess the highest level of comfort with the new technologies, are those who are the most vulnerable in the tenure and promotion system: assistant professors. Without concrete statements in faculty handbooks that clearly outline the type of scholarship in this area that would contribute positively to the tenure and promotion process, no institution will engage a significant slice of the faculty. The peer review process, which is unique to MERLOT, allows faculty to submit learning objects for review and review existing learning objects. The degree to which these activities should be judged to be equivalent to the traditional journal article submission and review process will be a matter of discussion for each institution, starting at the department level and moving up through each evaluation level. Our point is that these discussions must be initiated as part of the transformation process.

Reluctants

Although we defined this group as standing outside the transformation process, we believe that MERLOT offers a chance for engagement with at least some members of this group. Just as we have not yet encountered anyone who has made a serious attempt at word processing and then returned to the typewriter, we believe that exposure to the innovations and new ways of presenting material to those with a commitment to teaching might have a lasting effect. One method of doing this is to have departments hold a session where faculty are invited to explore the MERLOT site. We have found at these sessions that even the most skeptical faculty members tended to stay longer than the scheduled time.

Conclusion

The considerable number of challenges for higher education over the next five years will be easier to meet and overcome if administrators view the faculty as allies and collaborators. Faculty are not oblivious to the changes that are occurring in society at large, as well as in the halls of the academy. For the most part, they recognize that change is inevitable.

A possible threat to the ease of this transition lies with the process itself. The more that change agents and initiatives are tied to central administration and are seen as an imposition from above, as opposed to being the result of a constructive and collaborative effort, the slower the speed of change will be.

We encourage the following strategies:

- Conduct an assessment of faculty readiness that includes both their existing level of use and what they would like to do given the right conditions. Make sure you learn what they consider the "right conditions" to be.

- Make sure that faculty are included in any campuswide change process and that they understand that this inclusion is substantive, not symbolic. Make the fact of this inclusion as public as possible.

- Start an examination of how the institution's reward process should be changed to include faculty activities relating to the adoption of new technologies and professional activities done in connection with the technology adoption.

- Explore innovative, faculty-based resources, like MERLOT, that can facilitate change by connecting to several dimensions of what the faculty are doing and what they consider to be important.

- Examine the campus faculty support mechanisms, structures, philosophy, processes, and funding priorities, and adjust them to accommodate the mix of faculty groups on campus.

This is an exciting time to be involved in higher education; open communication with and meaningful engagement of faculty during the transformation process can create and spread enthusiasm for change.

References

Bates, A. A. *Managing Technological Change*. San Francisco: Jossey-Bass, 2000.

Blackburn, R. T. *Faculty at Work: Motivation, Expectation, Satisfaction*. Baltimore, Md.: Johns Hopkins University Press, 1995.

Brown, D. G. *Interactive Learning: Vignettes from America's Most Wired Campuses*. Bolton, Mass.: Anker, 2000.

Cahn, S. *Saints and Scamps: Ethics in Academia*. Lanham, Md.: Rowman & Littlefield, 1986.

Geoghegan, W. "Instructional Technology and the Mainstream: The Risks of Success." In D. Oblinger and S. Rush (eds.), *The Future Compatible Campus*. Bolton, Mass.: Anker, 1998.

Hagner, P. R. "Faculty Engagement and Support in the New Learning Environment." *EDUCAUSE Review*, Sept.–Oct. 2000, pp. 27–37.

Rogers, E. *Diffusion of Information*. (4th ed.) New York: Free Press, 1995.

2

Creating a Context for Consensus

David G. Brown, Sally Jackson

Every sort of practice within the college and university has been changed by the growth of the World Wide Web and related technologies. More profound change is highly likely, some of it unintentional. A central question for higher education administration is how to lead change in profitable directions and avoid getting committed to anything that could prove unhealthy for the institution.

Advice on directions is plentiful but inconsistent. Campus visionaries insist that investment in new technology will stimulate unprecedented organizational advancement, while other experts, both academic and technical, protest that organizational change should not be technology driven. Both public and private institutions face pressure from outside interests, again divided between proponents of technology spending and skeptics who doubt the return on investment.

Put as broadly as possible, the leadership challenge is not how to draw recalcitrant faculty into compliance with already chosen directions but how to cope with competing impulses within the campus community. How do we move from a position in which everyone has a different fixed idea about the changing higher education landscape to a position in which the community as a whole can move forward with confidence?

Two Cultures

Understanding the role of two powerful expert communities found on every campus is key to our purpose. We refer to the information technology (IT) community, whose members are mostly technologists, and the academic community, whose members are mostly faculty. Each community has its own distinct culture, with distinct values, and each of the cultures enjoys great prestige and intellectual authority when not in conflict with one another.

The two communities have clashed on the issue of how aggressively to push the incorporation of technology into teaching and learning. Despite the undeniable historical fact that many faculty embraced Internet technologies a decade or more ahead of the business sector and general public, IT professionals have regularly painted the faculty as resistant to technology and as obstacles to change—that is, resistant to the directions championed by the IT community. Faculty, for their part, have resisted pressure to invest time and money in unproven enterprises, and they rightly point out that those pressing for experimentation with unproven technologies are not the ones whose time will have been wasted if it fails. The two cultures are also hobbled with views of one another that prevent much influence of one by the other.

IT professionals believe in the transformative power of technology. Many are convinced that learning is less effective than it might be because we have not yet adopted enough of the right technology in the right places. They are advocates for greater investment in technology, greater use of technology, and more assessment of the impact of technology on learning.

Some faculty believe in the transformative power of technology, but most probably do not. Where teaching and learning are concerned, some fear that technology has the power to destroy teaching, not only as an activity but also as a profession, by reducing or eliminating personal (that is, face-to-face) contact between faculty and student. Individualized teaching and scholarship seem to IT professionals to be a luxury. They believe in work teams made up of diversified specialists, outsourcing, and joint authorship. Faculty culture is highly specialized but less reliant on explicitly negotiated team roles. Intellectual work in the academy is generally a lonely, solo enterprise, where the quality of work can be adequately judged only by equally specialized peers at other colleges and universities.

Because the IT culture is attuned to the integrated functioning of the whole organization, it is much more inclined to recognize the need for some organizationally legitimized decision making. In a world where choices are virtually infinite, technological innovators understand the importance of focus and of decisions that concentrate resources and effort.

Faculty culture, by contrast, is highly balkanized, a cacophony of specialized languages, with each faculty member speaking and thinking in idioms that relate more to the work of his or her discipline than to the general culture. Academics trust others who understand and speak their language. They live in a culture of local autonomy with each disciplinary subculture free to make its own choices about the value of any new idea.

Presumptions Concerning Change

One important point of similarity between IT professionals and faculty is a fascination with new ideas. Both cultures value creativity and openness to intellectual and material progress. However, even this key similarity provides only limited common ground for the concrete decisions to be made about technology, because the two cultures differ deeply in their presumptions concerning change.

Where change is concerned, two broad presumptions can be recognized as taken-for-granted operating principles of the two cultures. The first, known in argumentation theory as the *liberal presumption*, sees change as opportunity for invention and advancement and accepts large numbers of failed innovations as the cost of pushing forward. The second, the *conservative presumption*, sees change as something to be controlled through deliberation. Change must be justified in terms of something demonstrably wrong or in terms of some demonstrable benefit. (For a general discussion of presumptions, see Goodnight, 1980; for a discussion of the role of presumption in public argument, see Gaskins, 1992.)

For technology innovation and related issues of teaching practice, the conservative presumption demands evidence of benefit from incorporation of technology into teaching. Faculty operating from this viewpoint want to avoid wasting time on changes that will not bear fruit, and they tend to accept assurances of the value of change only from sources who clearly understand the demands of faculty work.

Technologists operating from the liberal viewpoint see experimentation not as a waste of time but as a necessary condition for innovation. Because they do not generally understand how faculty reason about the value of various professional activities, they often adopt strong secondary beliefs about the importance of changing the faculty reward structure to favor experimentation with new teaching practices.

Because of these presumptions about change, the two cultures differ in some striking ways that create actual or felt tension between them. Surveys of IT professionals commonly identify faculty resistance as a problem to be solved in moving their campuses forward, and faculty commonly complain that the IT organizations on their campuses are uncritical in their enthusiasm for every new trend. These differences in perspective are important to understand in the creation of a climate favorable to innovation.

Providing Leadership to Manage the Cultural Tension

Without some transcendent process or perspective, these differences generate irreconcilable expert opinion and impasse. Campus decision makers need to be able to look at technology issues from a broader view than that provided by either of these two cultural perspectives; they need to be able to understand why something that appears self-evidently desirable from one perspective can appear unde-sirable or even threatening from another. Even more, campus leader-ship needs to be able to define for itself a mediating role that uses this tension between two professional worldviews to encourage deeper re-flection on campus goals and strategies. Skillful management of dis-course can create an opportunity to elevate everyone's thinking through expansion of argument around the points of deep disagree-ment. Our problem is to set aside both presumptions about change and construct a discourse in which the burden of proof is evenly dis-tributed between proponents and opponents of any particular change.

For the conservative presumption, change is justifiable only once evidence is available for its benefits. This means that we have effec-tively ruled out change, because to get the evidence of benefits, we must first make a change. Ignoring the justifiability of technologi-cal innovation, the conservative presumption can be pushed to its limits by pointing out how it protects itself from dealing with any relevant experience.

For the liberal presumption, we have no way to predict the sweep-ing changes within an academic community that might result from changes that appear at first to be only technological. It is the un-known risks that remind us not to push an academic community be-yond steps that can earn authentic campus consensus.

Two basic rhetorical objectives for academic leadership, then, are getting all parties to understand that some level of risk is necessary simply to conserve our values under changing conditions and get-ting all parties to understand that some changes do not appear as im-provements *and in fact might not be improvements*. Neither change nor stability is presumptive: change is not assumed to represent progress, but neither is it held accountable to an impossible burden of proof.

Leadership Strategies to Consider Last, Not First

A dangerous but common framing of the leadership question is, "How can we get the faculty to do such-and-such?" How can we get the faculty to incorporate technology into the classroom? How can we get them to develop distance courses? This liberal presumption framing gives preference to one set of values, treating the activities as self-evidently desirable and the communication task as one of gaining compliance. When the communication task is seen as compliance gaining, the most common strategies are those that sidestep the difficult problem of changing beliefs: edict and incentive.

The dangers of edict are well known. Mandating that all faculty will have a Web presence for each course and requiring all faculty to develop distance courses are inflammatory actions to faculty. Faculty accept few mandates concerning teaching. Consensus on required Web publication of course materials is out of reach for now, given the many associated issues of academic freedom and intellectual property. Edicts that get too far ahead of faculty support for an idea are rarely successful, except in stimulating the invention of all kinds of clever strategies for noncompliance.

The dangers of incentive are subtler. Offering incentives to faculty to do what they do not value intrinsically has two disadvantages. First, it isolates individual faculty from their intellectual communities, inviting them to search elsewhere (for example, in faculty development committees and groups) for social support. This is exciting at first but does not usually offer the intellectual resources needed to sustain a disciplinary teaching and research program or the professional network needed to advance an academic career.

Second, it communicates unintentionally that the activities for which the incentives are offered are off the budget—outside the faculty member's full-time obligations. In research universities, the offering of incentives for extra teaching activity is practically certain to draw down research effort. And because these are more likely to attract faculty with flagging interest in research, they do little to elevate the prestige of the activity.

Incentives can be structured to avoid some of these dangers, but this requires a good deal of thought. Heavy reliance on incentives does not look as authoritarian as issuing edicts, but it has the same strong whiff of arrogance about it: the untested presumption that some new direction is desirable and the willingness to "get our way" without actually persuading anyone that our way is best.

Leadership Strategies to Consider First, Not Last

Neither the liberal nor the conservative approach appears attractive as a first-line strategy. What does appear attractive is persuasion occurring through critical discussion (that is, debate) with very broad participation offering diversity of views. This is not preliminary to change but a continuous process that creates conditions as favorable as possible to new thinking. The national Carnegie Campus Conversations project, for example, is designed simply to increase opportunities for faculty to talk about teaching (and about the scholarship of teaching), on the assumption that these conversations will produce a new consensus on the relationships among the professorate's various obligations.

Stimulating debate is not easy. It is unnatural to say, "I'd like to get us involved in a virtual university consortium, but let's see what the faculty think," and all too natural to say, "I'd like to get us involved in a virtual university consortium if I can just get some faculty buy-in." The questions animating discussion should be about goals, not means. Before figuring out how to participate in a virtual university, for example, we need to provide the opportunity to decide not to participate at all. This is especially true when administrative goals are far ahead of faculty consensus. Those visionary goals may mean that the leaders are exercising leadership, but it may also mean that they have overlooked issues of real concern.

How do we stimulate debate and other discussion? What we want is active private and public conversation about goals and values, and that takes place only when the issues themselves take hold. Issues are more likely to take hold if we frame questions to enlarge debate, avoid premature closure on any controversial issue, and participate as proponents rather than as judges.

- *Frame questions to enlarge debate.* Debate can be made narrow or broad, inclusive or alienating, depending on how its topic is framed.

Questions about change should be framed to accurately reflect the achieved consensus of the campus. Unless a university already has reached consensus on the desirability of virtual universities, "Shall we participate in the statewide virtual university?" is a better framing of discussion than, "How can we increase our ability to participate in the statewide virtual university?"

• *Avoid premature closure on any controversial issue*. Open, unrestricted debate is fundamental to science and scholarship, and in our scholarship we almost never close debate in any permanent sense. In practical affairs, we close debate when time runs out on a decision or when it appears that no further progress can be made. Usual means for closing debate are voting and adjudication. Although we should not expect to reach complete consensus on issues involving technology directions, we should be slow to close debate, slow to resort to votes, and especially loathe to make decisions that render further debate pointless.

• *Participate as proponents rather than as judges*. Leadership sometimes requires a risky personal commitment to a direction for change. Nothing we have said so far is meant to suggest that leaders should appear undecided when they have in fact formed an opinion about a direction for change. Addressing the campus as an audience to be enlisted into a standpoint is different, however, from addressing the campus as an audience to be informed of a decision.

Talk and Action

In identifying debate as a strategy to try first, not last, we may seem to be suggesting indefinite delays in experimentation with new technology on campus. That is not what we mean. We envision a strong communication component in every large or small step, making each practical task perform double duty as an occasion for education and persuasion, not just for faculty or for technologists or for administrative leadership but for all sectors of campus. To illustrate this, we return to the question of when and how to use incentives to change the faculty's calculations about what is worth doing.

A common strategy is to offer money or other goods in return for specific acts of compliance, and many instances of this strategy appear to confirm that it works. We have raised several objections to anything like this. We now point out how incentives can be structured instead to open up discourse around change while simultaneously moving forward in ways appropriate to the level of campus consensus on change.

Consider grants for instructional innovation. These look like a straightforward implementation of an incentive strategy and, moreover, like an incentive strategy geared mainly to innovators and early adopters. But this depends entirely on how the grant program is organized and what sort of discourse space it opens. Every grant program can do double duty for a campus as a communication campaign designed to draw attention to some particular set of issues. Understood this way, the design of a grant program becomes more important even than the amount of money spent.

Grant programs have several design features that can be tweaked to create much greater potential for stimulation of discussion—and to accommodate the differences in interest and value of the IT and faculty cultures. First, every grant program should have a recognizable issue agenda that proposers must address. Structured as proposal preparation guidelines, these present an opportunity for the designers of the program to raise campus consciousness about specific issues on which movement toward consensus would be desirable. For example, if a grant competition requires explicitly formulated theories of how the proposed innovation will affect learning, faculty accustomed to writing research grants to adapt to programmatic requirements will delve into topics in learning theory that they would otherwise never trouble to explore.

Second, every grant program should be understood as an opportunity to educate or influence a group of reviewers. The review panel should be considered an audience. What is most important in choosing this audience is not their competence to review, but the value to be gotten from their exposure to new ideas embedded in grant proposals. Showcasing funded projects is a good strategy for spreading innovations; involving a very large number of proposers and reviewers in talking about specific new ideas is a great strategy for spreading innovations.

Third, most grant programs should be made competitive, even when resources are not limited. This has two points: to communicate that experimenting with instruction is creative activity that may be judged qualitatively and to equip some segment of campus with knowledge and values needed to make quality judgments. Peer review is preferable in most cases, since it ensures that the work a faculty member invests in the activity is noticed and acknowledged by faculty colleagues. But even more important is the opportunity that peer review presents for movement toward consensus on the value of the activity and the dimensions along which it can be evaluated. In other words, a grant program should not simply select award recipients but should also educate faculty on how to evaluate innovation, so that creative teaching activity can also be recognized in other contexts, such as promotion and tenure.

Fourth, whenever possible, review processes should be designed to promote discussion. If grant programs are construed only as ways to distribute funds, a discussion-intensive review process will appear costly and inefficient. If grant programs are construed as communication campaigns, the reviewing itself is one of the most important events. Reviewing processes may be structured to promote or inhibit discussion. Having reviewers rate proposals and aggregating the ratings to determine awards does not stimulate discussion. Having reviewers meet to discuss proposals and make consensus-based recommendations is more effective in stimulating the sort of talk that leads to shared evaluations. Beyond the quality of decisions made, this review process gives every reviewer substantial new opportunities to talk about technology in teaching and to deepen his or her understanding of the state of the art.

Fifth, grant competition may be accompanied by broadly participative discussion of internal funding priorities. The process of deciding where next to spend money is an opportunity to draw together diverse members of the campus community to build consensus around a bigger picture. Including both technologists and academics increases the opportunity for both sides to articulate their abstract positions on change. For example, both change supporters and change skeptics share an interest in assessment.

What we have illustrated here for the design of instructional computing grant programs might also be illustrated for many other similar programs. The point of this discussion has not been that change can be stimulated through grants, but rather that any activity related to change can be structured to stimulate talk and support practical action simultaneously.

Conclusion

How we communicate is itself an important element of culture and an important determinant of the health of a community. We have argued here for treating the leadership of campus transformation as a kind of communication campaign, carried out with whatever resources (like grants) come to hand. But we have also tried to make a more subtle point: that leadership is responsible for creating conditions in which a campus may decide against change.

Belief in the transformative power of technology has certainly passed the tipping point in higher education. Not everyone agrees, however, that transformations through technology are desirable. Nor does everyone agree on what is to be transformed. We have no consensus, nationally or on most campuses, about even fundamental issues like whether to invest in classroom technology or distance technology—that is, whether to use technology to transform teaching and learning on campus or to use technology to support true anytime-anyplace learning. Proponents of the transformative power of technology frequently conflate these two possibilities as though they amount to the same thing.

These differences are not an obstacle to change in practice but an opportunity for two resourceful expert communities to improve and deepen one another's thinking. Until true consensus over directions is achieved, the most important task of leadership is to create conditions for serious, sustained critical discussion, occurring not before or after particular decisions but all of the time.

References

Gaskins, R. H. Burdens of Proof in Modern Discourse. New Haven, Conn.: Yale University Press, 1992.

Goodnight, G. T. "The Liberal and the Conservative Presumptions: On Political Philosophy and the Foundation of Public Argument." In J. Rhodes and S. Newell (eds.), Proceedings of the Summer Conference on Argumentation. Annandale, Va.: Speech Communication Association, 1980.

3

Managing Complexity in a Transforming Environment

Vicki N. Suter

In research fields ranging from evolutionary biology to condensed matter physics, complexity theory (Lewin, 1999; Cohen and Stewart, 1994) has emerged as a new metaphor for explaining the world. Complexity theory is a clear alternative to traditional scientific models, which explain phenomena in a mechanistic, reductionist, linear context. This prevailing scientific worldview has permeated social organization, and the modern structured, hierarchical organization is the result. These organizations are characterized by organizational boundaries, chains of command, strict job descriptions and roles, and formal communication protocol. We are all familiar and comfortable with such organizations, where basic organizational principles are based on command and control.

However, when the speed of change (in demographics, demand, workforce, technology, economics) leads us to the edge of chaos, the command-and-control model is not only counterproductive, it is simply not possible. The very strengths of command-and-control systems reduce a complex system's ability to adapt and react to rapidly changing conditions.

Managing complexity does not mean controlling complexity or eliminating it. It means tapping the power of complexity by accepting it, understanding its principles, and working with it as academic institutions work with faculty to transform teaching and learning.

This chapter offers a set of five principles for managing complexity in leading transformational change. These principles, which are derived from complexity theory, should all be applied simultaneously.

Principle 1: Give Up Control and Aim for Influence

Who "runs" the Internet? People looking for that mythical controlling body are stuck in the old command-and-control world. Peers (whether machines, institutions, programs, or system administrators) "run" the Internet according to common principles (communication protocols). In fact, the Internet is a powerful example of a successful complex adaptive system surviving and thriving without a manager.

Robert Axelrod and Michael D. Cohen (1999), as well as Philip Evans and Thomas Wurster (1999), contend that the original purpose of managers was to compensate for the asymmetry of information that characterized the pre-Internet world. Only senior managers had enough information to form and maintain the big picture, and the asymmetry of information increased the further one went down the organizational chart. Now the asymmetry is moving the other way.

In our new networked communications environment, the big picture is too big and changing too fast. The result is that everyone has to operate as an independent decision-making agent (according to commonly agreed-on principles). That is where influence comes in. Leaders can provide an environment with rich opportunities for everyone to engage in dialogue about purpose. As a result, everyone can understand and attach meaning in such a way that they manage themselves effectively according to agreed-on principles to achieve the common purpose. To bring this about, leaders have to convert their energy and focus from trying (futilely) to control to creating an environment that involves everyone in the system, all having access to the same information (and receiving training necessary to understand the information—for example, how to read a budget). Everyone also needs to share authority, responsibility, and the power to oppose. In this environment, information flows both ways. The more actively the local experts (faculty and staff) are involved, the better enriched the institutional vision will be, and the better defined the means to achieve it. It is the local experts who will have to implement the vision. (See Axelrod, 2000, for a detailed description of a methodology for creating this environment.)

In other words, the most important role of leaders is to give up control while ensuring that there are commonly shared principles for decision making aligned with the institution's goals. Most institutions, for example, have ceded the authority to subunits within the institution to develop and publish their own Web sites. The reason is that it is simply too complex to centralize such efforts and produce Web content that would be timely, useful, and accurate. However, total local control can also result in a chaotic Web site for the organization as a whole. An approach that provides institutionwide design guidelines and principles, and an institutionwide content organization framework (all developed through widespread consultation), will provide a healthy dynamic tension when combined with local control.

Leaders from institutions of higher education may be better positioned than others to create the right environment if they think of it as an adaptation of shared governance, where governance has been broadened (to be inclusive of the entire institution), focused (on defining common purpose), and accelerated (converted from a brake to an engine of change).

Principle 2: Study Your Campus Like a Work of Art

If we want to manage complexity in the sense of understanding it, we might think of each of our institutions as a set of patterns. To convert one set of patterns to another set (help the institution transform in order to respond to its environment), we have to have some way of studying the patterns as they are now and as they change.

Because every institution in every environment is unique, we must first make sure we can describe what the transformation will mean. Using the processes described for Principle 1, we have to create a new vision that people share, understand, and find motivating. The vision must also be what Thomas Angelo (1999) calls an "orienting vision." It must be a detailed picture that we can compare ourselves to at each stage of the transformation.

Once we have our own unique institutional vision for the future, we look closely at environments where a version of that vision is already being executed. Would these successes be reproducible in our institution? Would they scale? If they seem scalable, what indicators frame the success in measurable terms—that is, what led to the success, and what demonstrates the success? That sounds like assessment, and we are all wary of assessment; it can be a black hole for resources without much return. Nevertheless, a specialized form, transformative assessment, may be of use.

Angelo (1999) describes transformative assessment as follows: "To achieve transformation in higher learning, we must develop shared trust, a transformative vision of goals worth working toward, and shared language and concepts equal to the challenge. If we plan and conduct our assessment projects at every step as if learning matters most—and not just student learning, but ours as well—then the distance between means and ends will be reduced and our chances of success increased." Transformative assessment is based on looking for the circles of influence (where there is shared trust, shared motivation, shared language) that led to the success, understanding all we can about these circles of influence, and turning that understanding into a customized, pervasive assessment culture for our campus. We can think of it as looking at our campus as if it were a painting by Monet or a drawing by M. C. Escher—in other words, as a work of art.

The best way to look at a Monet is with a group of other people, in a room where you can get close to the work, then back off five feet, then thirty feet, and then go upstairs and look down at it, all the while talking over what you see with your companions (each of whom has his or her own perspective); finally, go back and look at it again a month or so later. That is exactly how our assessment cultures should function.

Monet did not see discrete objects; he saw changing patterns of color and light, and that is what he painted. Our assessment culture tracks the important patterns that repeat throughout the institution, monitors the development of the patterns, and experiments with what affects the patterns in ways that are in alignment with the campus vision and alters those that are not. Everything—people, projects, programs, departments—is evaluated on the basis of this common theme. Leaders need to communicate the information from this monitoring to refine the campus's understanding of the vision and continue to build shared trust, motivation, and language.

In a healthy assessment culture, attention is paid to outcomes *and* to the experiences that led to those outcomes; assessment is ongoing (not episodic) and involves everyone; and assessment is a part of a larger set of conditions that promote the desired changes (Astin and others, 1996).

Virginia Tech is an example of a university that has created such an assessment culture. For projects ranging from the community network to the Math Emporium, a new way of teaching mathematics that allows the institution to teach 30 percent more students with 6 percent less budget, assessment is an integral function. In the case of the Math Emporium, the project has been formally evaluated at three levels: internally by the math department, by the university, and by an independent assessment consultant.

Principle 3: Reduce and Reuse

Nature, that expert in managing complexity, has a way of creating useful structures and then using them over and over again for different purposes, and also of creating a common structure that many different processes can use. We can use this same approach for deciding how and where to invest scarce resources.

One way to apply this principle is to build structures that are flexible, robust, and responsive enough to be used for many purposes, for example, a telecommunications infrastructure that can carry voice, video, and data over the same wire. A computer systems architect calls these types of flexible, reusable structures *infrastructure*. Infrastructure does not have to be physical. For example, every software application running on campus could contain code to handle the question of what are you authorized to do once we confirm that you are who you say you are. Every system could require its own unique set of user names and passwords. It makes more sense to maintain one set of user names and passwords campuswide and a single application that authenticates who you are at the request of all other applications. Such an enterprise-scaled authentication infrastructure would mean that precious faculty time is not wasted in creating and managing student computer accounts.

The University of Michigan applied this principle by building such an infrastructure. In addition, instead of developing course Web pages one at a time for faculty, the university created a quick and easy way for faculty to build their own course Web pages using templates. Doing work that is reusable many different ways is the only way to respond to the tremendous technical support needs of a typical college or university campus.

A campus leader does not have to be a programmer or a systems architect to encourage this frugal approach to managing the complexity of technology. Campus leadership can make designing for reusability a basic value and principle by making it a funding requirement.

A nontechnical way to apply this principle is to use flexible organizational units that bring together the people with the talents needed to accomplish a specific purpose and then disband them once the purpose is accomplished. We call these organizational units *teams*, and the distributed control process by which each agrees to operate *project management*. Although the traditional organizational structure with static departments and units might be more efficient, the team-project approach is more adaptable and allows the institution to operate at a higher level of complexity. (For more on the team-based approach, see Chapter Six.)

Principle 4: Invest in Polyculture and Prototyping

Complexity models show that emergent order will be more adaptable if a diversity of agents and strategies is operating within the system. As defined by Axelrod and Cohen (1999), an agent interacts with its environment, operating in a particular setting and with particular capabilities and capacity for memory—carrying forward from the present into the future. People can be agents, but so can entire organizations, as well as nonhuman entities such as programs.

This principle says that in order to manage complexity by working with it, we need to build a polyculture. We need to do whatever we can to involve many diverse agents and experiment with many diverse strategies. This does not fly in the face of the arguments against boutique solutions made in Chapter Five if we provide a context for this experimentation by making sure that

- The scope of the initial experiments is limited to prototyping

- Prototypes are rigorously evaluated as to scalability and sustainability

- A distributed control process ensures that experiments do not slide into production without assessment and a go/no-go decision at the end of each stage: prototyping, technical feasibility testing, implementation feasibility testing, limited production, and then full production

The other essential shift is in understanding that a high percentage of prototypes fail in the traditional sense of the word, and each failure is necessary to create the conditions for the successful change.

In the higher education environment, many campuses developed course management systems to make it easier for faculty to place course materials on-line. If after two years the campus replaces such a system with a commercial course management system, was the home-grown system a failure? In the process of building these systems, the campus and commercial technologists learned much more about academic computing, the needs of faculty, and the way other campus systems needed to work with the course management system (for example, to eliminate the need for faculty to maintain class rosters if there were already a student information system that would do so). Faculty learned about the potential of such systems and started thinking about the new approaches to teaching that they made possible. Using the principle of polyculture and prototyping, the only way the home-grown system could be a failure is if the campus were still working on designing the perfect course system and had not put it into the hands of any faculty yet, or if the campus established it as an end point instead of a necessary step along the way.

Principle 5: Tap the Power of Limits

This last principle can be the source of our most creative work, but it is also the most difficult to embrace. Campus leaders must understand, communicate, and leverage realistic boundary conditions for their campus in order to bring out sustainable behaviors. We must give up micromanagement and fixating on either a technological or organizational end point and put our energies instead into guiding the system in the general desired direction, given the boundary conditions. The second principle—to study the campus like a work of art—directs us to make sure that internal signals and indicators are in alignment with both the general direction and the boundary conditions, so our organizations do not oscillate back and forth within the boundary limits.

A specific example of a boundary condition is that in order to sustain itself, a community must reuse and recycle all of its resources.

There is no such thing as waste; everything, including the by-products of another process, is used as a resource. If we think about that in the higher education context, we might see how we could begin to look at research not as an end point but as a process with by-products that could be used by other processes, particularly in support of teaching and learning. For example, at the University of Arizona, data collected for research projects about different aspects of the Southwest region (in research areas ranging from geology to ecology, biology, anthropology, and sociology) are being reused in student projects ranging from elementary school studies of the bioregion to first-year composition classes. The databases themselves benefit because if data are not used, they decay; if they are used, their accuracy and integrity tend to be higher, and the integrated view of the data across disciplines provides the potential for new research discoveries.

Conclusion

Janine M. Benyus (1997) synthesizes the ideas of complexity theory, chaos theory, and complex adaptive systems into a new scientific worldview called biomimicry, which "studies nature's models and then imitates or takes inspiration from these designs and processes to solve human problems." In her view, we can use nature as a model, a measure, and a mentor in order to manage complex systems. With our energies released from what has to be a doomed attempt to manage complexity through command-and-control methods, we can make good decisions by adapting Benyus's questions and raising them for every project, program, or technology:

- Is it sustainable—that is, does it use resources that will continue to be available, and only the resources it needs?

- Does it recycle and reuse everything that can be recycled and reused? Are its by-products useful?

- Does it reward cooperation?

- Does it encourage diversity by fostering polyculture and prototyping?

- Does it use local expertise?

- Does it curb excess from within?

- Does it tap the power of limits?

- Is it beautiful?

When we have established the right relationships in our complex and transforming environment, the results of managing complexity are paradoxically surprising and beautiful in their elegant simplicity.

References

Angelo, T. "Doing Assessment as If Learning Matters Most." *AAHE Bulletin,* May 1999. [www.aahe.org/Bulletin/angelomay99.htm].

Astin, A. W., Banta, T. W., Cross, K. P., El-Khawas, E., Ewell, P. T., Hutchings, P., Marchese, T. J., McClenney, K. M., Mentkowski, M., Miller, M. A., Moran, E. T., and Wright, B. D. "Nine Principles of Good Practice for Assessing Student Learning." AAHE Assessment Forum. [www.aahe.org/principl.htm]. July 1996.

Axelrod, R. *Terms of Engagement: Changing the Way We Change Organizations.* San Francisco: Berrett-Koehler, 2000.

Axelrod, R., and Cohen, M. D. *Harnessing Complexity: Organizational Implications of a Scientific Frontier.* New York: Free Press, 1999.

Benyus, J. M. *Biomimicry: Innovation Inspired by Nature.* New York: Morrow, 1997.

Cohen, J., and Stewart, I. *The Collapse of Chaos: Discovering Simplicity in a Complex World.* New York: Viking Penguin, 1994.

Evans, P., and Wurster, T. *Blown to Bits: How the New Economics of Information Transforms Strategy.* Boston: Harvard Business School Press, 1999.

Lewin, R. *Complexity: Life at the Edge of Chaos.* Chicago: University of Chicago Press, 1999.

4

Transforming Traditional Faculty Roles

William H. Graves

Explaining his uncanny knack for being in the right place at the right time, hockey star Wayne Gretzky gave us the concept of "skating to where the puck will be." This chapter is about skating to where the puck will be for higher education in the twenty-first century and the impact that e-learning—the use of the Internet in teaching and learning—will have on faculty roles in the future.

Technological forces of change are moving the higher education puck in a more transformational and disruptive trajectory than many faculty members might wish. Indeed, the convenience of Web-based access to learning opportunities and services—and the competitive advantages that can result from that convenience—are already propelling the puck along a path that is focused more on the learner than the instructor, a direction that dramatically veers away from the expected norm for many instructors. The opportunity for institutions of higher education is to bring these potentially divergent paths into convergence by working with their faculties to plan a

This chapter is adapted from William H. Graves, "Framework for an E-Learning Strategy," published in January 2001 by EDUCAUSE through the National Learning Infrastructure Initiative Web site at www.educause.edu/ir/library/pdf/NLI0014.pdf.

learner-centered path designed to achieve the social, cultural, and economic benefits that should be the goals of postsecondary education and training. Engaging and supporting the faculty in such an endeavor must be understood to mean helping instructors adapt the Internet revolution in human communication and resource sharing to increase the learning opportunities offered by their institutions, the convenience of the learning process, and the actual learning accomplished in that process.

Change in human affairs is typically incremental and mostly unwelcome. This is especially the case in faculty affairs, where the design and delivery of courses and curricula are generally assumed to be a faculty prerogative first and a response to market forces only second. But higher education has always had two expressions of value and practice: learning as a social good and learning as a market good. The latter is growing in importance in some segments of the postsecondary education market and thus must be taken into account in offering a sense of where the puck is headed. The trends toward learner centeredness and the competitive nature of market-driven education will have an impact on the role of the faculty even in the context of traditional colleges and universities.

Traditional higher education, although not one-size-fits-all as a marketplace, has primarily practiced an instructor-led, contact-hour course model. And there will continue to be a role for instructors in higher education. But that role is changing, even in the market for a residential general educational experience for young college-age students.

To understand the evolving role of the instructor in e-learning, we begin by examining the niche for formal instructorless learning, as small as it may be, and the real issue it raises: the relationship between self-study learning materials and instruction. We then explore the role of the instructor in learning and, especially, e-learning and discuss alternative paths for engaging and supporting faculty members on traditional campuses in the process of academic transformation.

Instructorless Learning

Even at the baccalaureate level, there are some precedents for rewarding instructorless learning with credit hours. Many colleges and universities, for example, award credit for selective levels of accomplishment on the Advanced Placement examinations, whether students studied on their own or in instructional programs offered elsewhere. And as the demand increases for continuing professional development, corporate training, and other forms of adult education, so may the demand for instructorless learning opportunities. Postbaccalaureate learning needs, after all, can sometimes be at odds with the instructor-facilitated course model, to the extent that instruction has a dominant same-time requirement and the learners are sufficiently motivated and self-reliant to learn on their own.

Indeed, with any capable and motivated students, comprehensive and effective self-study materials provide a powerful form of anyplace-anytime learning that can also be cost-effective, provided that the capital costs of developing study materials can be amortized at a low cost per student and that the need for instructional labor is kept to a minimum. Perhaps that is why some instructors are arguing against what they see as an instructorless future in which the courses they teach will be available for self-study on the Internet to generate revenue for their greedy institutional employers who forced them against their own long-term financial self-interests to develop these virtual (anyplace-anytime) courses. But it is equally likely that these same concerned instructors are confusing the publication of their content on-line with effective on-line teaching. Except in the circumstances involving highly motivated and well-prepared students who have learned to learn on their own, the delivery of content in any medium is seldom the sole component of an effective learning experience.

If on-line learning materials are to provide the opportunity for effective learning in a self-study environment, they must rise to the level of learningware, a software application informed by research in learning theory to provide structured opportunities for active learning. Learningware allows active decision making through simulations with parameters under the control of the learner, opportunities to create and interpret data, tutorial opportunities to react to spoken words or visual cues presented in a multimedia format, and so on. These ideas about content and the role of subject matter experts in the development of self-study learning materials have their traditional locus in the textbook.

The Role of Learning Materials in E-Learning

The anyplace-anytime textbook has long been a content mainstay that instructors use to organize a course of study and provide students with content material for self-study. Few instructors are textbook authors. Most select a textbook or similar content materials and prepare syllabi and lecture notes to sequence content, and they supplement that content with their insights.

Faculty can easily publish syllabi and lecture notes on the Web and in doing so may confuse this exercise with the electronic equivalent of authoring and publishing a textbook—a commercially viable, comprehensive explication of subject matter organized by the author's navigational logic for that subject matter. How else can the current furor over the ownership of on-line course materials be explained, when it is clear that institutions, not instructors, offer courses for credit and maintain official course records? Moreover, the posting of syllabi and notes on the Web usually happens without the peer review and professional editing associated with the publication of a textbook. The true technology-enhanced counterpart to the textbook is instead learningware.

Unlike the corporate training market for learningware as computer-based training applications, there is as yet no significant higher education marketplace for learningware. Substantive development costs, lack of learning technology standards, and return-on-investment issues associated with institutional adoption barriers in higher education still impede the development of highly interactive, media-rich learningware for the traditional higher education market.

Thus, most faculty and their institutions would be ill advised to enter the business of developing learningware, for internal use or for sale externally. A few faculty succeed today as textbook authors, and a few eventually may succeed as authors of learningware, probably by working outside their institutions and partnering with companies to develop such products.

Widespread commercial viability of learningware awaits a few more years of successful work by the nonprofit IMS Global Learning Consortium, Inc. (www.imsproject.org), which is facilitating the development and promotion of de facto standards for the "Internet architecture for learning" (Graves, 1999). The IMS standards are evolving to create a cost-justifying large open market for well-designed, highly interactive e-learningware for the higher education market. Only when this happens will virtual learning materials be on a par with virtual discussion, virtual tests, and virtual reference resources in terms of their efficacy. Even then it will be difficult for traditional campuses, whether operating in their traditional nonprofit modalities or through new for-profit subsidiaries, to pull together the creative teams, business teams, and investments required to create successful learningware unless they do so with experienced business partners in joint venture relationships. But experienced partners are likely to continue to differentiate the value of the individual subject matter expert from the value of his or her institutional employer, except possibly in the case of superstar professors and their brand-name employers.

In any case, engaging and supporting faculty in the development of learningware will be a selective and expensive proposition. Traditional campuses will need to learn to differentiate their potential role in the development of commercially viable learningware from their role in the development of virtual credential-conferring curricula offered to their markets. And the latter concept introduces the most common role in learning for most instructors.

The Role of the Instructor in Learning

Current punditry notwithstanding, content is not king in instructor-facilitated learning, and courses do not equate to content. Otherwise, colleges and universities would equate to (instructorless) libraries. If one calculus course can be differentiated from another, as many institutions that point with pride to their math programs might hope, it is not on the grounds of its content but through the efforts of the instructor. The importance of the instructor is relatively transparent, for example, when sorting historical final exam records by instructor in a multisection calculus course that uses a common textbook and a common final exam.

Indeed, instructors play a valuable role in student learning in higher education. Many students need the guidance of an instructor even when content is provided on the constructivist model to engage multiple senses and learning styles in self-study—as when exploratory, multimedia learningware is the vehicle for delivering content to learners for self-study. Instructors guide the acquisition of knowledge and help learners assimilate that new knowledge in the larger context of a coherent body of knowledge that constitutes a way of knowing—a curriculum, a liberal education, the scientific method, a body of professional knowledge and skills, and so on.

Instructors accordingly are seldom responsible for the development of content from scratch (learning materials) and, moreover, are responsible for much more than the delivery of content in fulfilling their primary responsibilities in organizing and managing a course. In most cases, instructors have a number of responsibilities:

- Selecting, sequencing, and supplementing topics (with class notes) from the "published" expression of content that is typically developed and copyrighted by others

- Facilitating discussions and other group activities to encourage active collaborative learning

- Guiding students' self-study through advising, tutoring, and assigning readings, papers, projects, learningware, and so on

- Critiquing, measuring (grading), and reporting their students' individual progress within an institutional or interinstitutional process that allows the appropriate institution or institutions to award credentials certifying a student's individual accomplishments

The Role of the Instructor in E-Learning

The new opportunities for anyplace-anytime learning appear to raise questions about the role of the instructor in e-learning. But are these in fact new questions? Almost any course, virtual or not, can be organized around a textbook or a collection of printed materials that present the subject matter to be studied, that is, the content. Digital materials increasingly can replace the textbook and other printed materials and can include class notes and even more extensive reading materials published to the Web. But the experience of reading these static materials in printed or digital formats, unlike the immersive learning experience that is possible through learningware, is often not a successful learning experience. That is why content has never been king in instructor-facilitated learning and why the second instructional responsibility of facilitating collaborative learning is a key to success in the instructional use of anyplace-anytime technologies, whether to enhance a traditional someplace–same time educational program or to create an anyplace-anytime (virtual) educational offering.

The point of this observation is to counter the prevailing notion that putting up course notes and static, noninteractive course materials on the Web results in an effective virtual course—a virtual correspondence course perhaps, but seldom a successful virtual learning experience. This simple observation should be factored into the development of any institutionwide strategy for e-learning. If it is taken into account, some of the current uninformed furor over course ownership and the future of instructors in e-learning should give way to an informed debate about effective practices in virtual education and related faculty development needs.

The net effect of the discussion to this point is that e-learning represents an opportunity to refocus the role of the instructor away from the delivery of content—the syllabus, lecture, and class notes in traditional terms—and toward the learning outcomes of instruction. From this perspective, the best instruction becomes a learner-centered activity that takes advantage of the convenience of virtual (anyplace-anytime) instruction to meet the learner's needs, which sometimes will have little to do with the enriching values that we associate with face-to-face interaction or other forms of same-time interaction.

Choosing a Path to Transformation

An institution may decide to use virtual technologies to strengthen traditional classroom programs or develop and deliver virtual curricula—or both. However it decides to use these technologies, it will need to provide professional development services to the faculty, either from inside or with assistance from an external partner. These services should focus on the use of virtual technologies in discharging the four fundamental faculty responsibilities already identified. Especially important in the absence of the contact hour is the faculty role in organizing and facilitating collaborative learning and, more generally, discovering effective methods for ensuring that the outcome of teaching is demonstrable learning in the context of working with others and assimilating, presenting, and discussing knowledge as an active learning event, with the student as apprentice scholar.

The breadth and depth of professional development services will probably vary with purpose. Few, if any, campuses will invest simultaneously in the development of a multitude of virtual curricula. Instead, most will focus on a few programs that are viable candidates for success and, in that context, will want to dedicate support resources to curriculum development. That development effort should include professional instructional design, in-depth technical support, and evaluation assistance for participating instructors in the interest of time to implementation, quality assurance, and initial and long-term success (see Chapters Five and Six).

Such in-depth attention to quality assurance and individual success may not be affordable when the goal is instead more focused on broad-based professional development than on strategic curriculum development. Broad-based professional development, for example, might be designed and supported with accordingly less support per instructor in order to encourage as many instructors as possible to enhance their classroom-based instructional efforts using Web-based technologies and to prepare them to begin to engage the possibilities for virtual instruction.

Each institution will need to consciously decide which paths to follow and allocate appropriate support resources accordingly.

Conclusion

The next few years will bring unprecedented instructional innovation, resulting in enterprise progress at some institutions but simply random acts of progress at others. The critical difference will be determined by whether an institution's leadership today is skating to where the higher education puck will be tomorrow.

Reference

Graves, W. H. "The Instructional Management Systems Cooperative: Converting Random Acts of Progress into Global Progress." *Educom Review*, Nov.–Dec. 1999, pp. 33–36, 60–62.

5

The Holy Grail

Developing Scalable and Sustainable Support Solutions

Joel L. Hartman, Barbara Truman-Davis

A major shift in the use of technology to support instruction oc-curred in 1995. Prior to that year, there was a general growth in the availability and use of various technologies on U.S. campuses. However, the 1995 Campus Computing Survey found that the use of instructional technology at all types of institutions was moving beyond early adopters and now including mainstream faculty (Green, 1995). Every Campus Computing Survey since that year has identi-fied the need to assist faculty in their efforts to integrate technology into instruction as the most important information technology chal-lenge confronting American colleges and universities over the next two to three years, with the second most important challenge being user support.

Technology adoption and support are necessarily intertwined. The tipping point at which the rate of adoption of an innovation begins to grow exponentially occurs when the mainstream faculty begin to become engaged in the transformation process. Once an innovation passes from the early to the later adopters, the size of the population that must be supported increases dramatically. In addi-tion, at the later stages of diffusion, there are large populations at multiple stages of adoption, bringing the new challenge of support-ing multiple populations with differential needs.

Faculty Support Models

Three models for supporting faculty in the use of technology are the lone ranger, boutique, and systemic approaches.

In the lone ranger approach, identified by A. W. Bates (2000), entrepreneurial or early-adopter faculty with a tendency to go it alone explore and innovate uses of technology in teaching and learning, independent of a structured support environment. Although this approach fosters faculty understanding of the potential of technology-assisted learning, Bates cites several negative characteristics of many projects developed by such lone ranger faculty: poor graphics and user interface, excessive technical time demands, failure to complete the project, and lack of dissemination of results. Self-direction can appear to work well for the innovator and even many early-adopter faculty because they are enthusiastic and self-reliant. However, such initiatives are heavily dependent on the ideas and energy of one or a few individuals, and they generally do not scale well as second-wave faculty become engaged throughout the institution.

In the boutique approach, one-on-one support to faculty is provided as they come forward requesting assistance. This is satisfying to both faculty and professional staff—until the number of faculty begins to increase. Dealing with an increasing number of individualized projects is certain to become a resource drain on faculty and staff time. In most institutional settings, such phenomena are likely to sound an alarm, sooner or later coming to the attention of senior administrators. Although boutique projects may be scalable, the support structure is not, eventually leading to the support crisis that many campuses are experiencing (McClure, Smith, and Sitko, 1997).

The third approach, systemic in nature, brings together campus support resources—including instructional designers, programmers, and digital media specialists—in a common strategy, supported by scalable systems and processes for dealing with rapidly increasing support needs.

The three basic support approaches are not mutually exclusive, nor is the existence of lone rangers and boutique support necessarily harmful. All campuses will have lone rangers; from these innovators come many excellent and creative ideas. To become scalable, the work of lone ranger faculty needs to be institutionalized and brought within the systemic support structure.

Boutique support is the optimum solution in many ways, and it might be preferred if not for its lack of scalability. But even in systemic support environments, boutique approaches are common. For example, as the systemic support organization begins to serve new faculty, a one-on-one approach is often used to assess faculty and project needs and to establish a trusting relationship. Individual faculty may also be identified as leaders and given special support to carry their innovative ideas forward. For example, at the University of Central Florida, we have established the Vanguard Faculty program especially for the purpose of providing boutique-like support for faculty whose special interests and talents can move the entire enterprise forward by creating scalable, sustainable models that other faculty can adopt.

The challenge in support is one of how to achieve scalability while maintaining quality as the number of faculty requiring support increases.

Characteristics of the Systemic Model

Systemic support models are characterized by five elements: faculty interest, administrative direction, facilitation, institutional capacity, and advocacy.

Faculty Interest

As Everett Rogers (1995) and Bates (2000) suggest, interest derives naturally from individual discovery and application of an innovation. The institution must create an environment that nurtures this interest in discovery. However, absent an institutional context and resources, interest alone is not sufficient to drive an innovation such as technology-enhanced learning throughout an institution.

Administrative Direction

Direction gives form and scope to technology-enhanced learning initiatives. It can come from institutional planning, from faculty-led initiatives, in reaction to external competition, as a means to improve teaching and learning, or as a response to student expectations. It can also come from leaders with vision and authority. Just as *interest* implies a bottom-up approach, *direction* implies a top-down approach. A top-down approach has advantages, such as securing a place on the institutional agenda and a heightened probability of resource allocations. However, lacking faculty interest and acceptance, administratively initiated efforts can be counterproductive, resulting in faculty avoidance or pushback. It is therefore desirable to have both faculty interest and administrative direction, with the two being in harmony.

Facilitation

Faculty interest and administrative direction may be insufficient to move an innovation through the institution; facilitation is also required. In describing facilitation, Bates (2000) lists components that are required to achieve quality in technology-assisted learning: content, media production, instructional design, and faculty and student support. The majority of institutions see a need to assist faculty with developing, delivering, and updating their on-line courses; however, the locus of this support may not be immediately apparent. Human resource issues include creating new and effective organizational models capable of accommodating the diverse range of expertise required to support mainstream faculty development, course redesign, production, and student support. How institutions can organize to facilitate instructional technology adoption is discussed in detail below.

Institutional Capacity

As the number of technology-assisted courses grows from the tens to the hundreds to the thousands, how will the faculty be trained, the courses created and maintained, and the increasing pool of online students supported? Processes that work well with the first few courses can begin to buckle under the weight of hundreds or thousands of courses. Therefore, one of the most important capacity issues is process scalability. Scalability encompasses both human and technological elements and requires effective processes and approaches. Supporting technology must be accessible and as easy as possible to use. Procedures should be designed to "teach faculty to fish" rather than "give them fish."

Advocacy

The final element of a systemic support model is the advocacy of one or more champions. Champions bring energy and direction. They help keep technology-assisted learning on the institutional agenda and facilitate communication among the various entities involved. Innovations that have credible champions disseminate more rapidly through the organization than those that do not.

The Need to Institutionalize Successful Approaches

The process of institutionalization is not unlike turning laboratory discoveries into successful products; it requires creating a link between the innovation and the institution's goals and directions. By creating this connection, the institution answers the questions, "Why are we doing this?" and "What do we want to achieve?" To the extent that innovations in technology-assisted learning support institutional goals and directions, paths are established that faculty can follow with some assurance of support and sustainability, and administrators can understand the resource demands of technology-enhanced learning in terms of institutional goals to be met.

The process of institutionalization has several key elements:

- *Accepted instructional model.* A generally accepted and under-stood model of instruction must be adopted as an operational base-line that becomes proposed practice. The model may be implicit and intuitive, but if this model has not been well researched, chances are that traditional practices of instruction will be used in the technology-assisted format. At the University of Central Florida, we adopted the Sorg-Truman (1997) model for our on-line courses and faculty development.
- *Standards and conventions.* Standards and conventions provide a road map and rules of the road that faculty can safely follow as they begin to adopt and subsequently master the innovation. Use of the plural form is not coincidental. The role of standards and conventions is not to pronounce one true way, but rather to reduce the range of possibilities from infinite to a sufficient and workable subset that the institution can realistically support. Standards include hardware (for example, PC or Macintosh), software (for example, WebCT), and similar choices that become the building blocks of the campus tech-nology effort. Conventions are established processes and procedures by which faculty and support staff employ these building blocks to cre-ate technology-assisted learning environments. The instructional model serves as a blueprint, and conventions enable consistent course construction and project management across varying disciplines.
- *Faculty development.* Providing faculty with effective instruc-tional examples to stimulate imagination and creativity, combined with training to help them master tools and conventions, increases the speed with which an innovation diffuses throughout the insti-tution. Strategic faculty development, especially when it is accom-panied by incentives and rewards, sends a message that the activity is important and legitimate and is a part of professional development.
- *Production support.* Making production support available rec-ognizes that most faculty do not possess the time or diversity of tal-ents required to create effective technology-assisted instructional

materials by themselves. Like faculty development, production support involving a team of instructional designers, programmers, and digital media specialists serves to increase quality and reduce risk, especially for nontenured faculty who must devote extensive time to research and publication.

- *Infrastructure.* Faculty development without infrastructure is an exercise in frustration. Infrastructure without standards does not provide a coherent environment, limiting the benefits of faculty development. Infrastructure must also be scalable and sustainable, that is, able to continue to be reliable and provide good performance as demand and users increase. It means, for example, buying servers that have more capacity than is required by existing demand, or machines that can be upgraded by adding in components or clustering. An innovation cannot diffuse throughout an institution unless the institution is prepared to continue providing the needed infrastructure. (Chapter Eight offers a more thorough discussion of infrastructure needs.)

- *Incentives and rewards.* Incentives are another sign of institutional commitment. These generally take the form of release time, direct compensation, funds that can be used for travel or student assistants, and hardware. While incentives draw faculty in, fostering adoption of an innovation, rewards recognize achievement. Whether in the form of recognition or success in achieving tenure or promotion, rewards confirm the safety and legitimacy of an activity.

- *Assessment.* In addition to finding out whether an innovation achieves the expected results, assessment can be of significant value as a means of continuous process improvement. In many cases, it is possible to blend assessment with innovative teaching, leading to publishable results or conference presentations.

Emerging Organizational Support Models

The rapidity with which interest in the new technologies is growing finds many campus support units scrambling to understand and

support the phenomenon. The information technology or computing organization may have extensive experience with Web-based
resources and services, but may not be accustomed to working with
faculty to develop and support courses and may have no pedagogical perspective to help it know which approaches are sound.

A similar dilemma exists for media services units, instructional
technology units, and campus teaching and learning centers. None
typically possesses the range of resources or skills necessary to support on-line teaching and learning fully.

Consequently, many campuses are finding it necessary to reorganize as a means of bringing to bear the expanded range of expertise and resources necessary to grapple with the needs of on-line
teaching and learning. At a minimum, needs include instructional
designers, HTML programmers, digital media designers, and producers, trainers, and systems support staff. As institutions begin to
reorganize, several alternative strategies are possible: add on to one
or more existing units, merge units, create a new unit, or outsource.
Combinations are also possible, and organizational needs may vary
between start-up and later activities.

An examination of the institutions that are regarded as leaders
in the distributed learning arena finds a new organizational model
emerging: one that is bringing together information technology and
instructional technology to develop scalable, sustainable support
strategies for technology-assisted teaching and learning. These units
may stand alone, or they may be an extension of other entities. This
model is characterized by bringing under one roof—sometimes in
the form of an instructional technology center—the range of expertise needed to perform the diverse tasks required to support on-
line teaching and learning.

A second characteristic of leading institutions and their new organizational models is the prominent role of instructional designers.
Often absent in traditional information technology organizations,
traditional teaching and learning centers, and media centers, instructional designers can play a dual role, working with faculty to de-

sign and implement effective technology-assisted instruction and creating professional development materials and training that support scalability and sustainability, reducing future support needs. The effectiveness of faculty development programs based on the central role of instructional designers often distinguishes institutionwide efforts from boutique efforts.

The Role of Instructional Technology Centers

Instructional technology combines the art of teaching and learning with the science of systematic development of technology-based processes and products. Thus, the knowledge base and staff characteristics within instructional technology centers usually include information technology specialists, instructional technologists (designers), and faculty.

When this work is done with academic programs rather than courses, the issues that must be addressed include the fundamental mission of the university (Dziuban and others, forthcoming). Typically, this is not within the purview of the instructional technology center, yet the success of programmatic initiatives is dependent on how well the institution knows itself and what it wants to become. Margaret Wheatley asserts that leadership must facilitate dialogue to determine what the institution could be (Katz, 1997).

To facilitate transformation, staff working within instructional technology centers must align their work with the institution's mission and become agents for changing not only the culture of teaching with technology but of the institution itself. A relationship exists between the degree of institutionalization of strategic initiatives and the existence of and adherence to a clear institutional strategic plan.

As instructional technology centers mature and effectiveness is illuminated by assessment, paths are cleared for faculty to follow, enabling greater creativity and experimentation. At the highest levels of development, instructional design and production support are offered. At the lowest levels, regular training is available to develop skills. Ideally, faculty expertise increases until a critical mass of adoption and dissemination exists, liberating the support staff to keep up with constantly changing technologies. In the interest of institutionalization, faculty should be neither totally dependent on support staff nor completely independent (lone rangers) but rather interdependent, doing what they do best and allowing instructional technology staff to provide support and peers to provide mentoring.

Recommendations for Action

What are some steps an institution might take to move toward an institutionalized, systemic faculty support model that will facilitate adoption of technology-based teaching and learning?

We believe that the key to achieving consistent quality and scalability is a coherent and comprehensive centralized support approach for course and faculty development. In the absence of an organizational unit that is able to provide the scope of support needed, such as an instructional technology center, establishing a coalition among existing instructional support units may be useful.

In such a coalition, course development units or teams work with faculty to prepare them and their courses; the computing unit can support the servers, manage networking and remote access, and provide help desk services; the library promotes student information literacy and ensures that on-line learners have access to the needed library resources. Balancing the multiple demands of on-line courses among multiple units distributes the burden, but it also requires close interorganizational cooperation.

In addition to addressing organizational needs, there are a number of other actions to take:

- Analyze what activities the institution does well but cannot scale, to determine if practices need to be reinvented or discontinued.

- Evaluate the effectiveness of training. Does it ultimately reduce the need for support despite increased numbers of persons trained or supported?

- Analyze the instructional innovations taking place in the institution. Where are they occurring? Are they random or systematic? What needs to happen to make these innovations more systematic, scalable, and sustainable?

- Analyze how your staff members spend their time. How much of what they do builds communities across the institution that lead to critical mass and transformation?

- Identify best practices that are scalable and sustainable, and showcase them through demonstrations or other events.

- Develop the means to systematically support the best practices that are widely adopted.

Conclusion

Transformation occurs when individuals, institutions, or processes undergo change that is so pervasive they are redefined and where such significant benefit results that they will not voluntarily return to the old ways. Transformation is unlikely to occur without all of the elements described in this chapter: faculty interest, administrative direction, resources, facilitation, and one or more champions.

Faculty interest develops only with success and can be sustained only if the continuing needs of the faculty are met. These needs include access to equipment software and faculty development, support for developing and offering courses, a reliable support network to insulate them from excessive technical demands, and rewards and recognition.

The existence of all of these elements requires an institutional commitment of some magnitude; however, if they truly support the institution's mission and goals, the return on investment can be significant.

References

Bates, A. W. *Managing Technological Change*. San Francisco: Jossey-Bass, 2000.

Dziuban, C. D., Moskal, P. D., Juge, F., Truman-Davis, B., Sorg, S., and Hartman, J. "Developing a Web-Based Instructional Program in a Metropolitan University." In B. Geibert and S. H. Harvey (eds.), *Webwise Design: Lessons from the Field*. Englewood Cliffs, N.J.: Educational Technology Publications, forthcoming.

Green, K. C. *The 1995 National Survey of Information Technology in Higher Education*. Encino, Calif.: Campus Computing Project, 1995. [www.campuscomputing.net].

Katz, R. "Higher Education and the Forces of Self-Organization: An Interview with Margaret Wheatley. *CAUSE/EFFECT*, Spring 1997, pp. 19–21.

McClure, P. A., Smith, J., and Sitko, T. *The Crisis in Information Technology Support: Has Our Current Model Reached Its Limit?* Boulder, Colo.: CAUSE, 1997. [www.educause.edu/ir/library/html/pub3016/16index.html].

Rogers, E. M. *Diffusion of Innovations*. (4th ed.) New York: Free Press, 1995.

Sorg, S., and Truman, B. "Learning About Teaching Through the Internet: Lessons Learned." Paper presented at the Society for Information Technology and Teacher Education Conference, Association for the Advancement of Computing in Education, Orlando, Fla., Apr. 1997.

6

Designing and Delivering Instructional Technology

A Team Approach

Gerard L. Hanley

The development and distribution of scholarship, teaching, and service to the institution are the three cultural elements of higher education. The balance of tensions among these three sub-cultures, their values, and their activities defines each college or university. These cultural tensions, values, and activities are powerful motivators for individual and organizational change. To integrate the design and delivery of instructional technology into an institution's culture, administrators need to leverage the momentum of that culture in positive ways, as well as change some of their institution's academic rituals.

The culture of scholarship is a core element of all colleges and universities, whether they are community colleges or doctorate-granting universities. The scholarship culture has institutionalized processes and resources to produce scholarly articles, books, and presentations. A goal of the scholarship culture is for individual faculty to produce high-quality and unique materials that contribute new knowledge to their discipline. Individual professorial applications of this model produce the markers that signify professional achievement in academia: tenure, promotion, and salary. It is only natural, then, that this traditional model of scholarship is now being applied to the development of instructional technology. The model is comprehensible and acceptable to the academic community and thus is usually at the heart of many institutions' initiatives, both technological and traditional.

The typical outcomes of this approach, however, include unpredictability in timely and quality results, inability to sustain or scale the project, little or no strategic application within the institution (the instructional technology is typically designed to meet the needs of only the individual faculty member's course), little or no acceptance by other faculty, limited accountability, and minimal use of the technology by students (Hanley, Schneebeck, and Zweier, 1998). Following the scholarship culture has led us to let a thousand flowers bloom, though most have died on the vine. If the goal is to achieve systemwide transformation, the institution needs to deemphasize individuated course development and support and move to a more team-based model.

This chapter presents a framework for designing new and using existing instructional technology to enhance student learning. The emphasis is on a coherent systematic approach to achieve scalable and sustainable results. Such efforts are essential if the goal is systemic transformation and not merely the cultivation of pockets of excellence. Experience at The California State University's Center for Distributed Learning (CSU-CDL) illustrates the success of the framework.

A Team Approach

An alternative to the scholarship model that is emerging within the instructional technology community acknowledges the success of team efforts. Team efforts can involve face-to-face contact, virtual contact, or both. Team efforts can be limited to a single campus community or can involve interinstitutional cooperation. The crucial skills within the team are content specialists, expertise in particular tools or programming languages, system integration and engineering, instructional and graphic design, usability, and project management.

Several kinds of changes are needed to embrace this new approach:

- Changes and enhancements to academic administration in order to respond to the requirements of team-based design processes.

- Changes in how the faculty view their teaching. The view of the teaching and learning process as consisting of the instructor, the instructor's assignments, and the students must give way to that of one where teaching and learning is the product of an integrated group of individuals, many of whom are never seen by the students.

- Changes in the management of the entire life cycle of instructional technology projects. These changes are useful in that they will reflect the undercurrent of systemic change, which is a fundamental principle of transformation.

Four Phases of Successful Design

Successful team-based design and delivery of instructional technology has four general phases. Scalable and sustainable systems require planning and support for all four phases. An institution's culture will require administrators to translate each abstract phase into concrete procedures. Following are examples of how the CSU implemented these phases.

Concept Development Phase

This phase focuses on defining and validating faculty needs for course enhancement using instructional technology and developing design team membership. It involves recognizing institutional needs and developing a consensus on strategic areas based on those needs. Institutional guidelines for defining the needs for instructional technology are critical and should be a central component of any request for proposals.

The CSU-CDL has developed and used standards and criteria for choosing proposals that have an excellent opportunity for success; they can be adapted for academic programs, campuses, and systems-level institutions.

- *Strategic applicability:* Addresses a priority academic concern and is consistent with the purpose and values of the institution's strategic plan.

- *Quality and quantity of learning:* Has a high probability of improving the quality of learning in clearly definable ways or will increase access to learning opportunities for a significant number of learners (or both).

- *Scalability:* Is planned and developed once, is shared or implemented on multiple campuses, and is adaptable for use by multiple disciplines.

- *Sustainability:* Can be supported through existing, stable sources of funding and approval processes and can deal effectively with the problems of technical obsolescence and need for continuous quality improvement.

- *Resource leveraging:* Uses new funding as a means of attracting additional investment from other sources, for example, redeployment of institutional resources, grants, and fundraising.

- *Multicampus participation:* Involves significant, active participation of persons from multiple campuses in planning, implementing, managing, and evaluating project activities. For a single campus, involving multiple units, schools, or departments would be required.

- *Timely results:* Provides early and continuous, measurable benefits.

- *Feasibility:* Can be accomplished within existing institutional, technological, and financial needs and constraints, including time frame and potential growth.

- *Acceptance:* Can be implemented in a way that provides for ongoing discussion and validation of the approach taken.

- *Accountability:* Provides academic, operational, and financial measures and metrics for monitoring the achievement of the project's objectives and outcomes.

Demonstration and Validation Phase

This phase focuses on developing proof that the proposed concepts can become real solutions. Working models of the instructional technology, pilot programs, or prototypes are developed and tested to produce evidence that the proposed solution has promise for success. Instead of selecting projects based solely on written proposals, the CSU-CDL has required that projects develop a prototype to demonstrate in front of a review committee. We recommend establishing review committees comprising people with the collective skills, knowledge, and experience required to produce good instructional technology. The committee should include faculty from a variety of disciplines and academic technology staff. Demonstrating the concept also focuses the review committee's evaluation on the possible achievement of a project's objectives in addition to its academic justification.

Detailed Design and Construction Phase

The focus of this phase is developing proof that the instructional technology will work well. It requires defining, producing, and integrating all work for the project's first-time implementation.

Two design control processes are critical for success. The first concern deals with the validation processes: Are we solving the right problem? The second process, verification, asks, Are we solving the problem correctly? Defining the right goals and performing regular assessment to see if the goals are being achieved are both critical processes.

The CSU-CDL has performed usability testing as a key design control process. Usability testing assesses four variables:

- Effectiveness of the technology to achieve the users' goals

- Ease of learning the technology by new users

- Ease of using the technology by trained users

- Preference for using the technology

Both validation and verification processes are performed at each stage of the design cycle and are critical in assessing whether the appropriate products are being developed correctly. To ensure that the management of the project is disciplined in following through on the design control processes, regular public demonstration of the progress of projects is important. Annual poster and demonstration sessions where funded projects show their efforts to the campus community are very effective and can lead to a broadening of faculty engagement as audience members are able to view concrete examples of new and innovative teaching applications. Faculty can include their presentations within their tenure and promotion portfolios as samples of their scholarship of teaching.

Production and Operation Phase

This final phase focuses on using the technology, including deploying, sustaining, and revising valued products. It has had the weakest support within higher education. Although the design of new instructional technology has many attractive features and is where a significant proportion of funds are allocated, the actual use of technology is the more critical activity and yet is the more critically underfunded. The scholarship culture does not reward the use of research to the same extent as the design of new research, and this bias applies to instructional technology as well.

Actual use of technology, not a theoretical discussion concerning the concept of its use, is what changes teaching and learning. Use becomes the field testing (verification and validation) of instructional technology.

Evidence of Effectiveness

Evaluation of use should include measures of access, ease of use, and achievement of student learning outcomes. The focus on use is consistent with the teaching culture, which involves selecting and repurposing others' work into a curriculum and pedagogy for effective delivery of an academic program. The faculty's skills and creativity involved in integrating others' materials to achieve student learning outcomes is critical. An international cooperative project such as Multimedia Educational Resource for Learning and Online Teaching (MERLOT, discussed more fully in Chapter One) is a free on-line resource designed to enhance faculty's ability to use others' instructional technology effectively and efficiently. Campus conferences and poster sessions for faculty reporting on their use of instructional technology can also be an effective means for sharing lessons learned and raising the recognition of faculty efforts.

Emphasis on and evaluation of instructional technology use can provide valid and reliable evidence of teaching-learning effectiveness. For example, usability testing can improve the quality of the technology project, and the systematically collected evidence can become part of the faculty's tenure and promotion portfolio.

The evaluation of the quality and use of instructional technology is an example of the scholarship of teaching and can produce publishable scholarship. This can serve as an effective means of engaging the reward seeker faculty member described in Chapter One. Absent evidence of effective use, evaluation of teaching with technology within the tenure and promotion culture will be difficult to change.

The university service subculture is the final area to leverage, with curriculum and program review committees playing key roles. These committees are often the units responsible for responding to the significant shift from teaching content to student learning outcomes. Curriculum and program review committees tend to focus on individual course content and less reliably on pedagogy (although it is the specific combination of content and pedagogy that produces student learning outcomes). Because content and pedagogy are intimately connected in instructional technology, program review and curriculum committees will have opportunities to develop institutional and departmental policies concerning content, pedagogy, and technology. These policies can guide the revisions of academic courses and programs.

Conclusion

In the past, the higher education classroom was in many respects an island unto itself, with very little influence from the outside world. Today, demands for assessment-based accountability have opened up the classroom for greater levels of scrutiny and demands for adherence to system-level standards, values, and goals.

The same holistic approach used in tying academic programs to college and university missions should be extended to the design of instructional technology. Both should be done in concert with institutional standards that are informed by the strategic priorities established by the institutionwide planning process.

Initiating and sustaining the team-based approach to the design and delivery of instructional technology requires coherent participation, accepted leadership, and recognized motivations for groups within the campus community. Leveraging the existing momentum of an institution's culture will be critical to overcoming inertia and promoting organizational change to sustain the systemic collaborations required for successful design and delivery of instructional technology.

Reference

Hanley, G. L., Schneebeck, C., and Zweier, L. "Implementing a Scalable and Sustainable Model for Institutional Software Development." *Syllabus*, 1998, *11*(9), 30–34.

7

Responding to Intellectual Property and Legal Issues

James L. Hilton, James G. Neal

American colleges and universities are seeking to extend and innovate educational programs through the expanded application of information and network technologies. Their distance-learning and electronically enhanced education aspirations are responding to new markets for networked learning.

The virtual campus demands significant digital content creation, new strategies for course capture and delivery, dependable and secure distribution and access systems, and new approaches to rights management. Whether working independently, in collaboration with other colleges and universities, in partnership with the private sector, or through spin-off entrepreneurial structures, all higher education institutions need to take a fresh look at the use and ownership policies that govern the working relationships with academic personnel. These include copyright and intellectual property, conflict of interest, conflict of commitment, and use of the institution's name.

The Association of American Universities' Intellectual Property Task Force (1999) argues that "the development of information technology and use of new media must be consistent with the normative code of the university" and that this embraces the elements of the open and free exchange of ideas, meritocracy, organized skepticism, and common ownership of goods. The report also argues that "the university should own the intellectual property that is created at the university by faculty, research staff, and scientists and with substantial aid of its facilities or its financial support."

The American Association of University Professors in its "Statement on Copyright" (2001) asserts what may be viewed as a contrasting or complementary position: "It has been the prevailing academic practice to treat the faculty member as the copyright owner of works that are created independently and at the faculty member's own initiative for traditional academic purposes" (p. 182). It notes the special circumstances of works made for hire, negotiated contractual transfers of rights, and joint works, all relevant to the on-line course environment.

A Shifting Copyright Environment

The debate over the ownership of on-line courses is taking place in the context of a shifting copyright environment. We are in the midst of a broad intellectual property revolution. The globalization of copyright through treaty agreements of the World Intellectual Property Organization (WIPO) seeks to harmonize national policies, and this is important for educational programs that increasingly seek to tap global markets.

Several important principles already cut across international copyright agreements. First is national treatment, whereby each country promises to protect the works of foreign authors the same way it protects the works of its own authors.

A second principle is territoriality, whereby one country's copyright law applies only within the country's border, thus producing significant differences from nation to nation.

A third principle is moral rights. In the United States, Great Britain, and other common law countries, copyright law reflects an economic character, offering the author or copyright owner (or both) economic incentives to encourage creativity and investment. Under the European model (also adopted in Latin America, francophone Africa, and Japan), the author's work is viewed as an extension of the individual. Moral rights include the right of paternity, which allows the author to decide when and how to first publish the work and the right to be credited as the author. There is also the right of integrity, which gives the author the legal right to prohibit the destruction of the work or a change in a work if it reflects negatively on the author's reputation.

Recent international agreements have spawned a series of important legislative initiatives in the United States. These include copyright term extension, the Digital Millennium Copyright Act (DMCA), the database bills (which seek to establish a new regime for the protection of facts), and the new Uniform Computer Information Transactions Act (UCITA), which, in the view of the higher education and library communities, advances the private law of contract over the public law of copyright.

Licensing has expanded rapidly as a tool for universities and colleges to negotiate the terms of use of software and access to electronic resources. Technological controls implemented by producers to manage access to computer information are advancing from passive password or IP (Internet protocol) domain models to more active encryption and self-help strategies. And writers and scholars are increasingly questioning through legal channels the right of publishers to recycle their works in new electronic publications or through document delivery, and in some cases they are asserting ownership or co-ownership of works being submitted for publication.

In the face of these significant developments, copyright in the United States retains several important and core characteristics. Copyright assigns to the owner of a work control or exclusive rights to prohibit others from using that work in specific ways without permission, and the ability to profit from the sale or performance of the work for a fixed period of time. These exclusive rights constitute a monopoly and include reproduction, distribution, adaptation, public performance, and public display. These exclusive rights granted to copyright owners are reduced, thus allowing limited uses, particularly if there are societal benefits. These exceptions or limitations are collectively referred to as *fair use*. In determining whether an action meets the test of fair use, four questions are typically applied: on purpose or character of use, nature of the work, volume of use, and the impact on the market.

Works may be copyrighted when they are fixed in a tangible medium of expression that can be perceived, reproduced, or otherwise communicated either directly or with the aid of a machine or device. An important test of copyright protection is the requirement that the work demonstrate a level of originality, something more than "merely trivial" variation and something that is more than "sweat of brow."

The concept of works for hire is important for determining ownership in an employment situation and is a central issue in the discussion of copyright and on-line courses. If a work is prepared by an employee within the scope of employment or is specified as a contracted assignment, the copyright law defines this as a work for hire and thus assigns ownership to the employer. In the United States, copyright ownership is typically assigned to the party that is in a better position to exploit the value of the work. Prior to 1976, copyright law, through an explicit teacher exception, treated faculty works as not works for hire. Whether the new copyright law has abolished this exception is an open question, for the courts have not directly confronted the issue.

Copyright Issues for American Higher Education

Many important copyright issues are raised in the rapidly shifting digital and network environment of higher education.

- Should U.S. copyright law be revised to harmonize with European and WIPO developments?

- How can fair use and access prohibitions be reconciled?

- Is an organization legally responsible as an on-line service provider for the acts of its employees and clients in the use of copyrighted information?

- Does the expanding use of digital and network copying and distribution require a new framework for copyright protection?

- Can an individual circumvent, for noninfringing purposes, the technologies that increasingly control access to computer information?

- Can the first-sale doctrine, which defines ownership and the right to transfer a work, persist in arrangements that are predominantly for the lease, rather than purchase, of information?

- What are the appropriate time frames for copyright protection, and how should this link with the potential for commercial exploitation?

- Can the uses of computer information and copyrighted works in the traditional classroom be extended to distance-learning settings?

- Is there a body of information that belongs to the public that should be available for use without copyright protection?

- Do we need database legislation that creates a new form of protection for factual information?

- Will the terms of contract agreements supplant copyright protections and the limitations on this exclusive right?

These are the legal and policy ambiguities that confront faculty and their colleges and universities as they create new courseware and build the virtual campus.

Principles and Roles for Colleges and Universities

Clearly, we are facing a period of severe copyright tensions, involving natural property rights, the fostering of creativity and innovation, public welfare interests, and public access needs. The creator, the distributor, and the consumer of a work are in conflict, and it is noteworthy that an individual may assume each of these roles at some point. The American higher education and library communities have adopted a set of principles that informs advocacy on copyright matters:

- Copyright law provisions for computer information and digital works should maintain a balance between the interests of creators and copyright owners and the public that is equivalent to that embodied in current statute.

- Copyright law should foster the maintenance of a viable economic framework of relations between the owners and users of copyrighted works.

- Copyright law should encourage ease of compliance rather than increasingly punitive enforcement measures.

- Copyright law should promote the maintenance of a robust public domain for intellectual property as a necessary condition for maintaining our intellectual and cultural heritage.

- Facts should be treated as belonging to the public domain, as they are under current law.

- Copyright should uphold the principle that liability for infringing activity rests with the infringing individual rather than with third parties.

- Educational institutions should foster a climate of institutional respect for intellectual property rights by providing appropriate information to all members of the community.

- New rights and protections should be created cautiously and only so far as experience proves necessary to meet the constitutional provision for a limited monopoly to promote the "progress of science and useful arts."

- Copyright enforcement provisions should not hinder research simply because the products of a line of inquiry might be used in support of infringing activity.

- Copyright law should ensure that respect for personal privacy is incorporated into access and rights management systems.

These principles were originally articulated by the University of California Task Force on Copyright in its final report and recommendations (1996).

The goals of American higher education are the development of policies for intellectual property management that enable the broad and easy distribution and reuse of materials by scholars and students and foster a competitive and supportive market for scholarly communication, learning, and creative work.

Universities and colleges have important roles to play:

- To provide knowledgeable expertise for their communities on intellectual property issues

- To act as political and legislative advocates for user interests

- To educate faculty and students on respect for copyright

- To have the required policies and procedures in place to respond to notifications of potential abuse

- To document the impact of changes in copyright laws on institutional success and quality

- To negotiate aggressively on license agreements

- To actively support new strategies for the ownership of intellectual property that protect the interests of education and research

How should academic institutions respond? It is important to recognize that copyright and intellectual property can be viewed from two perspectives: the lens of use and the lens of ownership.

The Use Perspective

The lens of use highlights the issues that arise when a person uses another's copyrighted material. Is it acceptable, for example, for a professor to put copyrighted articles on a Web site if access to the site is limited to students who are enrolled in the course? Can an instructor include another individual's tables and figures in a lecture? What if the lecture is being broadcast over the Web to students in a different location? How do the forms of the media (video, sound, image, text, software) and the methods of delivery (face to face, using the Internet, on CD-ROM, through television) influence a faculty member's choices in the use of copyrighted material?

Use-related questions are ubiquitous, and more often than not, institutions have been content simply to admonish their constituents to obey copyright laws. The problem with this strategy, however, is that copyright law is extremely counterintuitive.

To take just one example, the default assumption is that only works that carry the copyright symbol are protected by copyright. In fact, all works of original creation are protected by copyright from the moment they are fixed in a tangible medium (for example, written on a scrap of paper or stored on a hard disk). This means that handwritten notes, first drafts of articles, PowerPoint presentations, and virtually everything that one encounters on the Web is protected by copyright.

The surprising nature of copyright law means that institutions need to do more to help faculty, staff, and students understand the rights and limitations that come with copyright protection.

The Ownership Perspective

Whereas the use lens focuses on the use of third-party material, the lens of ownership highlights the concerns and questions that arise when members of the campus community create new pieces of copyrightable material. Ownership questions cut to the heart of the relationship between a university and its faculty. Anyone who raises the issue of who owns course materials will rapidly confront questions of academic freedom, scholarly tradition, and professional identity. Are professors more like independent contractors who work autonomously and should therefore own the rights to the material they create? Or are they more like private sector research scientists, in which case the university may own the rights?

Institutional policies that deal with ownership have not kept pace with changes in technology and academic practice. Many universities, for example, grant ownership of traditional scholarly works to the faculty while retaining an ownership interest in other intellectual property like patents. Two assumptions seem implicit in this position. First, scholarly works are less likely to involve significant institutional resources in their creation than are patentable inventions. Second, scholarly works can be defined more clearly and can be seen as the outcome of an individual's efforts. On-line courses are more complex in definition, often involving significant university investment in technology and teams of experts to create.

The Need for Institutional Policy Development

Although the use and ownership perspectives are not orthogonal, they provide useful lenses through which copyright and intellectual property can be viewed. Moreover, scholars, unlike publishers, do not have the luxury of thinking about ownership issues from only one of these perspectives. Both individually and collectively, scholars use the intellectual property of others and create their own intellectual property. From an institutional perspective, this schizophrenia means that a single solution is not likely to work. Instead, universities need to develop a suite of policies, tools, and practices to deal with the challenges that copyright and technology bring to the academy.

Most of the answers to the use-related questions come from interpreting the law and assessing the risk to the institution. Many of the use limitations come from outside the institution and are not under institutional control. However, a college or university can make choices that facilitate effective access, promote responsible educational use, and represent its interests and mission both locally and at the national level.

In general, institutions need to provide more guidance on issues of use. Faculty and staff typically do not know who owns what, who can use what under what conditions, or what they are able to do in their courses and scholarly work with either their own material or the works of others. The lack of clear guidelines can leave users confused and the institution vulnerable to litigation.

Pressures to create standard copyright use guidelines, particularly for electronic information, have thus far been widely and successfully resisted by the higher education community. But there is a need for reliable and consistent guidance at the institutional level on best practices in the use of copyrighted materials and for the nurturing of a culture of compliance. Similarly, faculty, staff, and students need to understand their fair use capabilities, when and how they should secure permissions, and when and how to secure alternative sources.

Institutions must define a comfort zone for risk. On the one hand, institutions that take an aggressive fair use position risk exposure to litigation and financial penalties. On the other hand, institutions that take a conservative position acquiesce to the increasing costs of access to knowledge and weaken the case for fair use that is now threatened.

University copyright policies typically fall short in dealing with new media created by faculty such as courseware, software, and Web sites, though many institutions are now aggressively reviewing and revising their policies. It is important that colleges and universities develop policies that recognize copyright as a bundle of rights, separate revenue sharing from ownership, focus more on the use of institutional resources and less on the type of property created (for example, textbook versus software), and align ownership with the academic values and institutional mission.

Ownership policies should be principle based and well articulated, with minimal ambiguity. Overly broad assertions of institutional ownership will alienate faculty and ultimately undermine the creative and collaborative environment. The reports by the Association of American Universities and the American Association of University Professors already referred to are excellent and provocative policy papers, and recently revised intellectual property policies like those at the University of Chicago (1999), Columbia University (2000), and Duke University (2000) illustrate different institutional approaches.

In addition to reviewing the institution's intellectual property policy, it is important to review other policy areas as well: conflict of interest and the ability of a faculty member to work with competing institutions or private publishers, conflict of commitment and the time that a faculty member devotes to carrying out academic responsibilities, and the use of the institution's name and advertising. The policies must articulate the mission of the institution to create, preserve, and disseminate knowledge and must acknowledge the responsibility to protect the interests of both the creators and the institution while guaranteeing that society benefits from the distribution of this knowledge.

Policies should outline clearly the purpose, scope, and authority for the policy and provide a glossary of terms. They should distinguish between sponsored research and copyright ownership for independent and directed efforts, patents, and other types of intellectual property while describing the responsibilities of the creators and the institution. Joint appointments, private sector collaborations, early disclosure, revenue sharing, and dispute resolution are just several examples of other issues that should be covered.

Clark Shores (1996) outlined an early and productive scheme for looking at these issues in the context of faculty creation of computer programs, multimedia works, videotaped lectures, and distance-learning courses. It asks these basic questions:

- Will the institution assert ownership and, if so, in which works, by what means, and through what process?

- Will ownership be defined by broad classes of materials, by the extent to which institutional resources were used in preparing the work, the commercial character of the work, the utilitarian versus the scholarly nature of the work, or the connection of the work with the faculty member's job responsibilities?

- Will the means be a blanket intellectual property policy, an employment agreement, or a contractual obligation?

- Will the process be assigned to a university copyright office, the university counsel's office, or a peer copyright policy and oversight committee?

The Rush for Web Space

James Neal (2001) points out interesting and important parallels between the push of colleges and universities into cyberspace and some noteworthy aspects of U.S. economic history. The current rush to stake out Web space for educational enterprise is comparable to the nineteenth-century land rush experience. The massive economic benefits of the railroad and the transformations it engendered in so many industries align with the impacts of electronic commerce in many areas.

The extreme fragmentation, and later rapid consolidation, of utility industries such as electricity and telephone might predict a similar winnowing at some point in the on-line education industry. We now see many layers developing around educational commerce, including numerous educational destinations for on-line courses, many new education portals or pipelines that aggregate offerings, and new business-to-business sites serving on-line learning. For colleges and universities to compete successfully in these markets, new entrepreneurial approaches to the geography, psychology, and economics of innovation will be required.

American higher education is challenged in this competitive market that increasingly is attracting new for-profit players. Universities and colleges must be able to support the educational needs and demands created by employment transitions and career changes and the needs of nontraditional students who are now the majority—students who are juggling families, jobs, and education. They must begin to view the undergraduate degree as a step and not the termination of an educational relationship with a student, and graduate learning as leading to a process of ongoing and global consultation and collaboration. They must be able to deliver high-quality and flexible learning into the corporation and the factory, and to forge educational partnerships with the K–12 community. Each of these thrusts will require new thinking about how to support teachers and learners and about the information resources, instructional content, and collaborative tools they will require.

Conclusion

How will higher education acquire sufficient infrastructure, quality courseware, willing faculty, comparable student services, enterprise management tools, new delivery models, and meaningful assessment strategies? How will higher education successfully implement advantages of on-line learning such as interactivity, flexibility, functionality, cost of access, and support for diverse learning styles? And how will it forge a new partnership with faculty to advance this expanded agenda? All will require a fresh look at the copyright and other legal policies that underpin and serve the educational enterprise as well as fresh approaches to the use and ownership aspects of intellectual property.

References

American Association of University Professors. "Statement on Copyright."
   In *Policy Documents and Reports*. Baltimore: Johns Hopkins University
   Press, 2001. [www.aaup.org/spccopyr.htm].
Association of American Universities, Intellectual Property Task Force. "Intellectual Property and New Media Technologies: A Framework for Policy
   Development at AAU Institutions." [www.aau.edu/IPReport.html]. 1999.
Columbia University. "Columbia University Copyright Policy."
   [www.columbia.edu/cu/provost/docs/copyright.html]. 2000.
Duke University. "Duke University Policy on Intellectual Property Rights."
   [www.duke.edu/web/ost/invention/docs/IntelProp.pdf]. 2000.
Neal, J. G. "The Entrepreneurial Imperative: Advancing from Incremental to
   Radical Change in the Academic Library." *portal: Libraries and the Academy*, Jan. 2001, pp. 1–13.
Shores, C. "Ownership of Faculty Works and University Copyright Policy."
   Association of Research Libraries Newsletter, Dec. 1996.
University of California Task Force on Copyright. "Copyright Legislation and
   Scholarly Communication Basic Principles." In *Reports and Recommendations*. Oakland: University of California Office of the President, 1996.
   [www.ucop.edu/irc/wp/wp_Docs/wpd006.html].
University of Chicago. "New Information Technologies and Intellectual Property
   at the University." [www.uchicago.edu/docs/policies/intell_prop.html]. 1999.

8

Form Follows Function

Establishing the Necessary Infrastructure

Bret L. Ingerman

I f you were asked to describe the technology infrastructure of your institution, where would you begin? Regardless of whether your institution is of the traditional bricks-and-mortar variety or virtual, you would probably start by describing the network. Such a response would fit in well with the dictionary definition of *infrastructure*, which is "an underlying base or foundation." But the description should not stop there.

For an institution to move toward technology-enhanced education, whether dealing with students on campus or those at a distance, the required infrastructure goes well beyond the ubiquitous network that is now assumed to be in place on most campuses. Infrastructure also includes classrooms and other types of learning spaces, library and digital information resources, course management systems, high-end display devices, high-speed connections in residential and learning spaces, not to mention faculty who use the technology-rich learning environment and information technology (IT) staff to provide twenty-four-hour support to students and faculty. Failing to include these types of assets, both physical and organizational, neglects the second dictionary meaning of *infrastructure*, which is "the basic facilities, services, and installations needed for the functioning of a community or society."

This chapter is about the infrastructure required to create an engaging teaching and learning environment in the networked world of higher education. It explores the facilities and organizations that are needed to support the technological needs of an institution's learning environment, suggesting a series of questions to ask in any examination of existing infrastructure and in planning for its growth and adaptation.[1] Although the discussion is primarily geared toward traditional institutions, many of the issues presented lend themselves equally well to a discussion of a virtual environment. And although many of the issues raised have direct relevance to the World Wide Web, their relevance goes beyond this specific technology. The Web may be just the current step in the evolution of communications technology; there could well be an equally transformational technology in our future that we have not yet envisioned.

What Have You Already Built?

Transition strategies should leverage existing infrastructure whenever possible. Before you know where you are going, you need to know where you are. Just as you need to assess the state of faculty adoption of instructional technology, as suggested in Chapter One, so should you inventory your technology infrastructure—not only physical assets but also organizational assets. An assessment of existing infrastructure, including administrative support systems, hardware, software, classrooms (overall quality of the space, existing equipment, network connections, and so forth), and number and technical expertise of support staff, will reveal how far and how the institution needs to move along the transition continuum.

Examining Assets

With respect to physical assets, a good place to start is by examining the learning spaces that already exist. The definition of *learning space* is subject to local interpretation, but in its broadest possible sense, it includes any location where teaching and learning takes place. On traditional campuses, such spaces certainly include classrooms, seminar rooms, conference rooms, and laboratories. Including library study rooms, residence hall rooms and lounges, and even faculty offices can add to an understanding of the types of learning activities that occur on campus and how the technology infrastructure is supporting those activities.

In addition to taking stock of physical assets, you should inventory the organizational resources that comprise the technology infrastructure. What groups and individuals are responsible for the physical, technical, and scheduling aspects of learning spaces? Are these activities relegated to individual units, or are they a shared responsibility?

This is a good time to assess the adequacy of staff resources and support structures. Such an assessment would include the level of expertise of technical staff and the size and skill distribution of such staff. Among the possible assessment questions are these:

- Do network support staff have an understanding of contemporary issues (such as wireless technologies)?

- Does the network operations manager understand the role of the network in facilitating teaching and learning?

- Are there a sufficient number of network staff with the appropriate range of skills to provide twenty-four-hour support service to faculty and students?

The institution also needs to examine staff training policies and programs. Many technical staff require ongoing training to stay abreast of changes in the technology, especially networking.

There is as well an emerging need for professional-level instructional design and development staff to work with faculty on new modalities of teaching. These staff members often work in professional teams with networking experts and instructional technologists. The institution must determine if it has a solid cadre of such personnel distributed across these areas of expertise.

In too many instances, such staff members, if they exist at all on a campus, are beleaguered by demands for services that they are unable to render owing to outdated support structures and unrealistic expectations. Too often, institutional staffing and support practices are designed to meet the needs of a small number of entrepreneurial faculty rather than those of the rapidly growing numbers of second-wave faculty, students, and staff.

Assessing How You Support Your Assets

It is risky to assume that the institution is providing an adequate level of technical and physical support. The types and levels of support being offered may be a matter of perspective, differing between those seeking the support and those providing it. We have all encountered situations where we see the same problem day after day: the classroom PC does not work; the network is slow; the technology provided is too complicated; the expected technology does not exist in the assigned teaching space; the equipment is inadequate for the pedagogy.

Among the support-related questions that should be asked are these:

- Who should be reporting these problems, and are they actually being reported?

- Do people know to whom to report problems and how to report them?

- Do the people receiving the information have the authority, resources, and knowledge to act on it?

- Are the same people as in the past responsible for dealing with today's learning space problems and inadequacies, and if so, do they understand the transforming environment?

The answers to these questions indicate the extent to which the institution has aligned action with rhetoric.

Assessing the level of financial support is also critical. You must know whose budgets are involved in maintaining your assets and how those budgets are determined. In addition, you need to identify how many different pockets must be sought to perform both minor and major repairs and who must approve spending on minor and major issues for facilities and staff. Knowing whether there are cyclical renewal plans in place for the institution's physical and technical assets is also important. All educational transformations will engage every aspect of the financial structure; knowing how that structure works is critical.

What Do You Need to Build?

As form should follow function, so too should infrastructure follow need. The next step is to determine what is needed and why.

Establishing Institutional Goals

Any planning for the facilities that the institution needs to support its academic mission must be done in the broader context of institutional goals and objectives. For example, how many students should you be planning for, and what will the student population look like? Will they be traditional students, or will they be communicating and learning using electronic means? These choices, however, are not always exclusive. More and more faculty and students are coming to the institution with the expectation that they will use the network to engage in active learning experiences, collaborate, form learning and social communities, access information resources, and learn independently. Moreover, some institutions have a residency requirement for distance learners that can affect their classroom use, especially for technology-capable facilities. Other institutions are exploring the use of on-line courses for residential students to meet high demand or to accommodate scheduling problems (since such courses are often self-paced).

What level of technology use do you see for your students in the short and long term? Many schools either have in place an information literacy requirement or are discussing the creation of one. How does, will, or should such a policy affect students?

Will the institution be requiring students to own a computer and, if not, is the expectation that the majority of students nevertheless will have one? Reading assignments are predicated on the assumption that each student has a copy of the textbook. How would faculty change those assignments if they knew that there was only one textbook for every ten students? The nature of student assignments in a technological age, then, is intimately related to whether students will have their own computers with the necessary access to networked resources (including digital library resources) or whether they will be sharing public computer labs.

How do faculty plan to use technology? How many will need instructional design and technical assistance in revising their teaching styles? An equally important question concerns the classroom experience and what it should be like (and what students are increasingly expecting it to be like), especially in the light of available technologies. There is no question that we are moving from a "sage on the stage" model to one of the "guide by the side," leading to an increasing need for smaller, more flexible learning spaces on campus.

The institutional challenge is to reconcile the fact that the network allows learning to occur anytime and anyplace with the expectations that are designed into the physical plant. Flexibility should be the design concept of campus infrastructure. In addition to physical learning spaces, the ubiquitous network, wireless connectivity, and appropriate access on and off campus are essential aspects of the overall institutional learning environment. All students, as well as faculty, should have access to an Internet service provider (ISP) and a computer for their personal use. There are a variety of ways that this can be accomplished, from institutional hosting of such a service (the institution is the ISP) to having the faculty and students secure this service on their own through a commercial ISP. Individual institutions must determine their technical and financial role in facilitating such faculty and student access.

What about the nomadic nature of students? The institution will need to consider wireless technologies so that students can carry their computers from room to room, lounge to lounge, and indoor to outdoor while maintaining connectivity. Group study locations should have projection equipment and seating that allows students to work cooperatively on computer-based presentations. If we are truly to embrace the concept of anywhere-anytime learning, we will need to make sure that all facilities can accommodate modern technologies or, at the very least, that they do not present a barrier to them. This means that the institution will need to develop a transition strategy that moves from a focus on physical space to a concept of learning that occurs in a distributed environment, that is, anytime, anywhere, and anyhow.

Restructuring Academic and Administrative Support Systems

What is the future role for campus administrative departments in an increasingly technology-based educational environment? Distributed learning brings with it the expectation that faculty and students will have the ability, for example, to document learning outcomes; locate, use, and pay for learning objects; and create learning portfolios.

It is becoming possible to provide faculty, students, staff, and even parents with ready access to information that previously required a personal visit, or at the very least a telephone call, to obtain. Yet simply providing information is not sufficient. The trip to the registrar's office not only provided information; it also provided an explanation for how that information could be used. How can or should this be replicated in an on-line environment?

Complicating this is the fact that students expect that the information will be synthesized and presented in a way that reflects how they want to use it. The student does not care that the registrar, library, academic department, and bursar maintain their own information, are located in different parts of the campus, and report to different areas of the administration. Students want to see degree audit information alongside class schedules, syllabi, and curricular support materials, all on-line and in one place. Such expectations are not unreasonable, given their experiences with Web-based information resources and businesses.

At first blush, many would think that an on-line environment simply requires a more sophisticated technology infrastructure. Although this is true, many institutions have a long history of designing fault-tolerant, redundant systems for critical on-line applications such as e-mail, administrative information systems, and, more recently, World Wide Web servers. Combining these practices with the new crop of course management tools can provide a strong foundation for a virtual learning environment.

Since the costs of creating and supporting these on-line courses are substantial yet sometimes hidden, it is important to leverage the installed base of hardware, systems, and good practice whenever possible. Executive-level discussions of investments in new technical infrastructure should always address the issue of leveraging what currently exists.

Institutional standards for hardware and software—for example, an institutional course management system—are likely to be necessary to help contain support-staff costs and provide faculty with the independence they covet in their pedagogy. Other options include contracting with a vendor for such course management services. Reasons to consider outsourcing can range from the determination that local staff are insufficient or inexperienced, to the desire to move very quickly into new educational markets. Moreover, a growing number of vendors of course management systems are entering into relationships with vendors of administrative systems to provide their institutional clients with a fully integrated support package. The cultural, political, and philosophical dimensions of such outsourcing decisions are perhaps more significant than the technical and financial.

Supporting Distant Learners

If the institution decides to offer courses to students located at a distance, questions of support immediately arise. One of the greatest impediments to student success with distance learning is the technology itself. How will the university provide support for distant students, especially when that support is usually required after normal business hours? And more than technical support will need to be provided.

Academic support from the faculty and support from and access to the library are critical elements. Many campus libraries are staffed to handle the workload associated with students coming in for reference help, yet what happens when the library receives requests for assistance from students working off campus? Who will identify and make certain that the distant students have access to appropriate digital library resources or if such resources even exist? Access, over the network, to the appropriate array of supplementary information resources is too often assumed or overlooked.

Institutional leaders have an obligation to make certain that learners have access to all of the library and service resources to succeed in the course no matter where the student is located.

Envisioning the Learning Environment

Knowing what the goals are for the institution can help in determining how many classrooms and other learning spaces are needed and how they need to be configured. Although it is important to realize that the technology should not drive the discussion of classroom configurations, it is also the case that technology can no longer be relegated to a few multimedia auditoriums or be thought of last when it comes to planning and budgeting. Faculty and students are bringing technology into every space on campus, so it is prudent that discussions focus on the overall design of all campus spaces.

It is one thing to design learning spaces that assume students will be physically located in them. It is quite another to design facilities for distributed education. Distributed-learning classrooms may require more sophisticated audio and video systems than traditional ones. If these facilities will be used to communicate with students who are learning at a distance, they will require a substantially different type of infrastructure that may tend to make the facility look more like a television studio than a classroom. If, however, the faculty member will be teaching to a local audience at the same time as the distant audience, then the technology will need to be more tightly integrated to accommodate the more traditional design. On the other hand, the learning space for distributed education could also be a cybercafé, a residence hall room, or the campus quadrangle.

Although some faculty will desire every classroom to have all forms of technology available, such a design strategy may not be financially practical or prudent. Other faculty may bristle at the need to use twenty-five thousand dollars worth of technology "just to show overheads." In fact, too many bells and whistles could make the technology more threatening to such faculty. A reasonable short-term but evolutionary approach is to design a technology stratification for the campus that categorizes classrooms by the degree of technology that is required to be permanently installed versus that which should readily be accommodated. Thus, a basic classroom may contain a television, a videocassette recorder, and overhead projector. An expanded basic classroom might provide digital video disk (DVD) players, as well as slide projectors. Perhaps a premium classroom could be divided into *full-serve* and *self-serve* models. A full-serve classroom could have computers, visual presenters, and sound systems, all accessible from a central podium and a wireless mouse. A self-serve premium classroom could have some of the technology readily available, such as projection and amplification, while requiring a faculty member or IT staff member to deliver a laptop computer or DVD player as needed.

The learning environment also should include the ability to move from lecture, to discussion, to collaboration on the network, to independent Web-based research, whether the learning is taking place in a classroom, residence hall room, home, or someplace else.

On campus there also need to be spaces equipped for teleconferencing and presentation practice. Students and faculty expect and need twenty-four-hour access to the network and the associated staff support.

With respect to network connections, will classrooms be wired, wireless, or neither? Wired classrooms allow for most laptops to plug in and get on-line, but they require a sophisticated infrastructure of data and power cables that goes to each seat. Wireless technologies hold the promise of removing the networking wires, but what about electrical power? To some extent, the answer to these questions depends on the location of the campus and its physical construction, as well as the technical competence of support staff.

The introduction of new technologies often generates unanticipated problems—for example: Will students be required to charge their batteries before class and, if so, what happens if their batteries die in the middle of a class (or, worse yet, during an exam)? Wireless technology also currently requires most students to invest in special networking hardware. Laptops of the future will undoubtedly have this capability built in, but what do students do until then? A more basic question would be: Will the furniture in the classroom accommodate a laptop in addition to the other materials that the student is required to have? And what about students who do not have laptops?

After deciding the mix of classroom spaces and the level of technology that is appropriate for each, attention turns to other areas of classroom infrastructure. In full-serve premium classrooms, how does the faculty member use the equipment? Is she required to turn on eleven different pieces of equipment before she can use the technology, or is there a single integrated interface that requires only a press of a single button or a touchscreen? If there is a touchscreen, what happens if it is not working? Are the support staff located conveniently so that it only takes a few minutes to respond to problems? What training is in place to show faculty members how to use the technology and how then to integrate it into their teaching? Is there sufficient notice as to which faculty members will be teaching in these rooms to be able to show them what the room is capable of and train them appropriately? The institution's infrastructure transition strategy should include a quick transition to technologies with intuitive interfaces. Not all faculty like to train to be able to teach with technology.

Updating Residence Halls

What should residence halls look like? Technology has given us powerful asynchronous communication tools that promote the idea of anywhere-anytime learning. Colleges and universities increasingly are requiring, either explicitly or implicitly, that students make use of their computers outside the classroom. For the majority of residential students, the "anywhere" is the residence hall and the "anytime" is most likely after 5 P.M. and on weekends, both of which have significant infrastructure implications for the campus.

Older residence halls pose a significant challenge to the successful incorporation of technology. Many institutions have borne the cost of providing data networking, if not to each resident then at least to each residence hall room. Yet network access is only part of the problem. In many of these rooms, there is insufficient access to electrical power, a situation that leads to extension cords snaking across and around the room. If a student is fortunate to have access to power and to data, it is often the case that these connections are not located near the built-in desk. Furthermore, many student work areas are too small and too poorly designed to serve as both a writing surface and a place to house a computer.

Who Needs to Help Build It?

Much of what occurs on campus with respect to the support of infrastructure is due to the ad hoc coordination of a number of groups, each responsible for a small piece of the puzzle. Such an approach will not meet the needs of ever more complex facilities located in ever more diverse settings.

The stakes are high. We are in a period of rapid transition that is likely to result in the transformation of the institution. Institutional leaders face governance and financial challenges to implement an effective planning and decision-making framework for technology. The key stakeholders on campus for planning, supporting, financing, and using new facilities need to be consulted in the spirit of shared governance.

The key point here is that the right infrastructure is essential to the fulfillment of the institution's mission. The related decisions are as much about institutional values and culture as they are about the technology. That realization is central to the understanding of who must participate in and own those decisions.

The days of relegating such matters to physical plant staff, the campus architects and designers, or the technology staff are gone. Infrastructure is a leadership matter, and higher education leaders must become conversant with the issues insofar as they relate to the destiny of the institution. The art form of higher education leadership today is to design an executive advising council, for example, a president's cabinet, that includes the chief information officer and whose deliberations address matters of infrastructure as they relate to institutional mission, culture, and governance. Everyone at the table has a stake in infrastructure decisions.

Conclusion

There is a need to reconceptualize the notion of the institution of higher education as a destination for learning. The concept of infrastructure has changed to include the digital environment provided by the institution. The Internet has liberated both the learner and the faculty member from the confines of place.

Instead of assuming, "If we build it, they will come," or asking, "If we build it, will they come?" we should be designing and building infrastructures such that we can say, "If we create the right learning environment, they will want to be part of it."

Note

1. Readers will find additional questions concerning academic technology infrastructure in the on-line *EDUCAUSE Guide to Evaluating Information Technology on Campus* (www.educause.edu/consumerguide). Although this guide was developed to help students and their parents evaluate IT as part of their college selection process, many of the questions can provide valuable insight to institutions seeking to assess their IT infrastructure's readiness to support technology-enhanced learning.

9

Assessing Conditions
for Campus Transformation

Carole A. Barone, Paul R. Hagner

Technology, especially the Internet, is creating a new context
for higher education that college and university leaders cannot afford to ignore.

- Students increasingly are considering the state of an
  institution's technological integration in their application and acceptance decisions. An institution's lack of
  engagement in the transformation process will likely
  translate directly into lower enrollments.

- Faculty now coming into the profession possess more
  sophisticated teaching and learning technological
  capabilities. An institution that does not offer an environment that allows them to use these skills might
  not be able to attract them (or retain them if they do
  accept an offer).

- Skillful integration of new technologies into teaching
  and learning improves the quality of institutional
  course offerings. Avoiding such integration indicates
  lack of administrative adherence to a model of continuous improvement.

These emerging conditions call for new governance conventions, designed to involve faculty strategically and viably in decision

making in a competitive higher education marketplace that requires quick and decisive action. However, there has been a tendency on the part of the leaders of traditional campuses to dismiss discussions of academic transformation and distributed learning as being applicable only to institutions with adult learners or distant learners as their primary target markets or to the growing for-profit sector of higher education. These institutions run the risk of failing the very students who flock to the traditional residential setting.

Faculty are detecting new forms of cognition on the part of students entering traditional higher education institutions (Brown, 2000; Frand, 2000). For this reason, there is an exploding number of faculty members in need of assistance in revamping their teaching modalities to relate to these new learning styles. Moreover, recognition is growing that knowledge is becoming increasingly fragmented and indeed being created in new ways from information stored and accessed on the Web. Consequently, even on the traditional residential campus, the classroom is no longer bounded by four walls with a single faculty member in command of the distribution of information and the imparting of knowledge. Precisely for these reasons, all higher education leaders must confront the emerging realities of electronic learning environments.

Patterns and Findings: The Need for Institutional Leadership Strategies

During the first eight months of 2000, the National Learning Infrastructure Initiative (NLII) held a series of three focus sessions to advance the level of thinking on engaging and supporting faculty in technology-enhanced teaching and learning. Participants included academic administrators, faculty, chief information officers, instructional technologists, and others.

Many arrived at these sessions believing that the key to institutional transformation was faculty engagement in the challenges surrounding the role of technology in such transformation, along with faculty participation in local decisions about the infrastructure needed to support the adaptation of individual pedagogy to a new teaching and learning reality. Participants in the focus sessions thought that the challenge was to convince faculty that they had to change their way of teaching to take advantage of technology's power to provide greater access to higher education (through distance learning) and to the learning material itself (through the development of customized learning environments). They were convinced that the need was to educate faculty to participate thoughtfully in the decision-making processes surrounding these issues on their campuses. Furthermore, they thought the need was to convince faculty, technology staff, instructional designers, and instructional technologists that they needed to work collaboratively to produce learningware.

To some extent, the participants believed that the outcome depended on faculty respect for the professional expertise of support staff and on the support staffs' recognition of the personal and independent nature of teaching. They assumed that faculty engagement in the challenges would ultimately result in the requisite realignments in support structures, budgets, and technical acquisition practices.

Indeed, these variables associated with faculty engagement and support do contribute to the overall ability of an institution to move to a new context within which to pursue its mission. However, what emerged from the NLII focus sessions was a clear indication that the only way to transform gracefully is to ensure that the process is institutionwide. Those who participated in all three focus sessions recognized that a pattern had developed in the conversations among participants from all types and sizes of institutions represented in the discussions.

That pattern is reflected in the "Twelve Campus Conditions for Transformation" developed by Carole Barone (2001) from the NLII focus sessions. We believe these twelve conditions (see Exhibit 9.1) must exist for a college or university to be able to sustain and scale support for faculty who commit to accommodating new student learning styles and new institutional goals for distributed learning.

Exhibit 9.1. Twelve Campus Conditions for Transformation

- *Choices:* Identifying a strategic direction and selecting a path to get there based on a clear sense of institutional mission

- *Commitment:* Allocating resources and aligning policy to enable the institution to adjust its course and follow the selected path

- *Courage:* Providing visible and focused leadership from the very highest level of administration

- *Communication:* Building a climate of trust by including the entire campus community in the transformation process through a carefully conceived and well-executed strategy for consultation (conversation and critical discussion) and for dissemination of information about extant and emerging services, plans, decisions, and so forth

- *Cooperation:* Collaborating across functions and throughout levels and constituencies to achieve a consistent and integrated set of support services for teaching and learning

- *Community:* Complementing the community of support nurtured through cross-functional collaboration with an equally cohesive community of faculty across disciplines; creating an engaged community of learners

- *Curriculum:* Reconceptualizing the curriculum to reflect its distributed, interdisciplinary, and outcomes-oriented nature

- *Consistency:* Reflecting institutional commitment to transformation through consistent action and acknowledging the importance of standards, both within the technology industry and the institution; aligning organizational rhetoric to support and reinforce transformative behavior

- *Capacity and competency:* Developing "the teaching and learning capacity of the institution (for example, curriculum and faculty) to serve student achievement and outcomes" (Council for Higher Education Accreditation, 2000, p. 3); using intelligent assessment to drive transformation by defining and evaluating institutional success in terms of student achievement and outcomes

Exhibit 9.1. *(continued)*

- *Complexity and confusion:* Overcoming the confusion associated with coping with transformation by adapting to the inherent complexity of the decision-making process and adopting more agile and responsive governance processes
- *Culture and context:* Understanding the culture, values, and sensitivities of the campus climate
- *Creativity:* Developing strategies and tactics that harmonize with the campus culture and context and recognizing that this is a creative, not a political, process

Source: Barone (2001).

Coupled with decision-making tools such as the Conceptual Framework for Distributed Education and the Institutional Readiness Topology (www.educause.edu/ready/), these conditions provide the basis for informed, realistic, and viable decisions.

Together, the twelve conditions describe a contextual web for decision making that is inclusive in assigning ownership of issues involving technological infrastructure. Until recently, it has been common practice for institutional leaders to pass off decisions regarding such infrastructure, including support for teaching and learning, to their institution's chief information officer (CIO). Even if the CIO has sat at the president's or chancellor's table, matters of technology have rarely been entertained at that level. Consequently, technology-related decisions (and their consequences) have been perceived to belong in the province of the CIO. Such practice has been both convenient and attractive—convenient because it allows leaders to avoid the effort to acquire some competence around technical issues and attractive insofar as it allows leaders to skirt responsibility for the inevitable tensions that arise from the change enabled by technology. Thus, for example, an attempt to discuss the implications of a gigaPoP connection has been more likely to elicit giggles around the executive table than any thoughtful exploration of the consequences for the institution's instructional program or research portfolio.

To complicate matters even more, as information technology continues to become more specialized, fewer and fewer CIOs will come from the faculty ranks. Without that experience, decisions regarding the application of the new technologies to the teaching and learning process, not to mention the tenure and promotion process, will be less than well informed. This puts the CIO in the uncomfortable position of being handed a policymaking authority with no guidance from above and no experience from below.

Applying the Twelve Conditions for Transformation

Higher education faces a growing number of students who expect to participate actively in the creation of knowledge in a distributed-learning environment, an even faster growing number of faculty who want to create new learning situations for their students, and unprecedented external competition.

The twelve conditions for transformation set the stage for a new style of higher education leadership that includes owning responsibility for linking infrastructure to academic strategy within the unique value system, culture, and worldview of an institution. It is unrealistic, unfair, and unwise to relegate such decisions to the CIO. With this background, the twelve conditions take on strategic relevance.

Choices

The institution must be ready to make technical choices based on a clear sense of institutional mission. Chapter Eight tells us that infrastructure decisions need to be linked to overall institutional goals and strategy. Although technologists must participate in the deliberations surrounding such choices, integrating technology into the institution's sense of purpose should not be left, as it has been so often until now, to the futile efforts of campus technologists. Moreover, failing to consider the consequences of technical decisions for institutional direction is a decision in itself, made at the very highest level. Chapter Eight also conveys a powerful message about the responsibility of institutional leaders to participate in answering the difficult questions about purpose when contemplating changes to the institution's infrastructure.

Commitment

Institutional leaders indicate commitment to a strategic direction and awareness of the role of technology in executing that strategy by allocating resources and aligning policy to enable the institution to adjust its course and follow the path selected. This commitment must be able to bridge the philosophical divide outlined in Chapter Two, while maintaining the flexibility and ability to adapt covered in Chapter Three.

Courage

Such actions require courage, that is, visible and focused leadership from the very highest levels of administration. Lip-service no longer projects commitment; courageous action is required. Leaders must be willing to confront the nettlesome and complex legal issues outlined in Chapter Seven to protect the interests of both the individual staff and faculty member, as well as the rights of the institution itself. Systemic efforts such as those advocated in Chapter Five demand tough decisions concerning the allocation, not to mention reallocation, of institutional resources. Without clear support from the top and a willingness to make these calls, the effort will fail. While transformation necessitates grassroots support, it is not in itself a self-generating process.

Communication

Building and nurturing a climate of trust to support strategic choice requires communication. Communication in this context means much more than the dissemination of information. It means the adoption of new techniques for including the stakeholders in discussions about the transformation process through a carefully conceived and well-executed strategy that artfully meshes education with consultation. Chapter One argues that the effective communication of success stories can play an important role in faculty engagement. Chapter Two offers some creative strategies for engaging the campus community in addressing these critical issues by suggesting that leaders pose the key questions early and unassertively. Chapter Three provides some reassuring ways of perceiving and orchestrating the seemingly chaotic and rapid consultations surrounding the momentous decisions that are now endemic to the transitioning higher education enterprise.

Cooperation

Cooperation generally goes hand in hand with executive ownership. Clearly articulating the institutional goals with respect to teaching and learning and then linking those goals to the components of the implementation strategy (for example, changes in policy, new structural arrangements, infrastructure requirements) will set the stage for collaboration (Duin, Baer, and Starke-Meyerring, 2001). Cooperation across functions and throughout levels and constituencies is necessary to produce a consistent and integrated set of support services for teaching and learning—for example, the collaboration of the chief financial officer, CIO, provost, and faculty leaders in reallocating funds to implement a course management system for Web-based learningware. The team approach to support described in Chapter Six is built on the collaboration of many dedicated individuals who come with discrete skills to build a collective outcome.

Community

Community is created differently in a networked world. Students use the Internet to create electronic communities that fulfill their need for social interaction and serve as a source of information in the social learning context that many students value (Brown, 2000). To nurture a community of learners, a community of support created through cross-functional cooperation needs to be complemented by an equally cohesive community of faculty across disciplines. Community is thus enabled and supported by the network and is essential to the ability of the technology to support the community's existence. Chapter Three's suggestion of viewing an institution like a mosaic, where the individuals can blend together to form a unified whole, needs to be considered seriously.

Curriculum

Reconceptualizing the curriculum to reflect its distributed, interdisciplinary, outcomes-oriented, and, in some cases, distributed nature is integral to transformation. Such a reconceptualization flows naturally from the linkage of goals, strategy, and infrastructure with institutional culture and values. It is, however, vitally dependent on the self-awareness and attitude of the faculty in relation to their role in institutional transformation. Supplying faculty with new hardware and software and expecting them to use them automatically to transform their teaching is akin to adding more yeast to a recipe and expecting to produce more bread (Ehrmann, 2001).

Hardware is but one of the ingredients in the transformation of the teaching and learning process. Faculty awareness of the new reality and their attitude toward it will largely affect the extent to which institutional policies support or thwart intra- and interinstitutional sharing of courses and curricula, integration of the disciplines across the curriculum, and flexible learning contexts—for example, on-line versus classroom-contained teaching and collaborative learning. Institutions must grapple with the tentativeness produced by the conservative philosophy outlined in Chapter Two. This means that support structures must go beyond the technical and embrace the pedagogical.

Consistency

Consistency has not, until recently, been a required attribute of either an institution's instructional support program or its leadership's response to transitional adaptations. Indeed, survival often depended on the leader's ability to finesse decisive commitment to any one direction, approach, or standard. Institutional commitment to transformation will be reflected through its ability to establish consistent course support systems and practices and its willingness to acknowledge the importance of standards, within both the technology industry and the institution. For example, while collectively higher education institutions play a key role in the work of the IMS Global Learning Consortium, Inc., to establish industrywide standards for interoperability among hardware and software products for teaching and learning, individual institutions might select a course management system for Web-based learning, invest funds to participate in consortia such as the Multimedia Educational Resource for Learning and Online Teaching (MERLOT) repository, and align organizational rhetoric to support and reinforce such actions. As Chapters Five and Six point out, the boutique approach can work against systemic transformations because of problems relating to scalability. The resultant technological tower of Babel leads to desert wandering rather than constructive success. The absence of a consistent support framework serves to surface evasive leadership tactics.

Capacity and Competency

These conditions assume a reconceptualization of the curriculum to develop "the teaching and learning capacity of the institution (for example, curriculum and faculty) to serve student achievement and outcomes" (Council for Higher Education Accreditation, 2000, p. 3), as well as to use intelligent assessment to drive transformation by defining and evaluating institutional success in terms of such achievement and outcomes. This implies a major shift in focus from assessing quality based on inputs to the teaching and learning process—for example, faculty achievements, student Scholastic Aptitude Test scores—to assessing quality based on student competencies and certifications. As Chapter Four argues, faculty will have to incorporate these new conceptualizations of success and failure into the restructuring of their course offerings; although this process may be difficult, the new measures bring their own distinct rewards. Obviously, major tensions arise from the conflict in values attendant to such a shift. The spirit of cooperation and mutual ownership can help diffuse such tension so that the academic community can critically consider the implications.

Complexity and Confusion

An exercise as simple as running through these twelve conditions quickly surfaces the complexity and confusion that abound in our minds and emotions regarding these issues. One method of adapting to the complexity and confusion associated with interrelationships inherent in decision making during major transition is to adopt more agile and responsive governance processes. This is an important early step. Many of the tensions, sensitivities, and frustrations arise from the incompatibility of extant governance conventions with the exigencies of decision making in the emerging new higher education context. Attempts to preserve such processes are as futile as trying to administer around them.

Culture and Context

As Chapter Three points out, the key stakeholders need to begin to come to terms with the fact that norms and conventions developed in the context of the industrial age are losing their effectiveness in dealing with the time frames and complexities of decision making in the information age. Part of that coming to terms is fitting new processes into the existing institutional culture and context.

Creativity

Making these delicate and essential linkages requires not only an understanding of the culture, values, and sensitivities of a given campus climate but also creativity in developing strategies and tactics that harmonize with the community's perception of itself. Understanding the motivations of the actors is a first step. Chapters

One and Two argue forcefully that actions are the product of values and underlying philosophies. The challenge for leadership is to use the constructive components of these worldviews to produce collective action. This is as much a creative as a political process; a tad of understanding of social anthropology might also be helpful.

Conclusion

The twelve conditions embody far more than a checklist to determine a campus's readiness for transformation. The core message conveyed in these conditions is that technology must be employed within an overall sociotechnical system. Policy and practice with respect to the role of technology must be conceived, and perceived, to fit within the institution's culture, values, and style of operation.

In conceptualizing the place of technology in this way, the entire institution participates in, and owns, the transition enabled by the technology instead of being threatened by and hostile to it. Such widespread engagement demands a new breed of aware and engaged leader.

The twelve conditions for transformation cannot occur in a leadership vacuum. In selecting presidents and chancellors to lead higher education institutions in the information age, boards of trustees would be wise to evaluate candidates in terms of their awareness of and attitude toward these conditions for transformation.

References

Barone, C. A. "Conditions for Transformation: Infrastructure Is Not the Issue." *EDUCAUSE Review*, May–June 2001, pp. 41–47.

Brown, J. S. "Growing Up Digital: How the Web Changes Work, Education, and the Way People Learn." *Change*, Mar.–Apr. 2000, pp. 10–20.

Council for Higher Education Accreditation. *The Competency Standards Project: Another Approach to Accreditation Review.* Boulder, Colo.: National Center for Higher Education Management Systems, 2000.

Duin, A. H., Baer, L. L., and Starke-Meyerring, D. *Partnering in the Learning Marketspace.* San Francisco: Jossey-Bass, 2001.

Ehrmann, S. "Model Assessment Programs and How You Can Get Involved."
    Paper presented at the Fourth Annual Ubiquitous Computing Confer-
    ence, Seton Hall University, South Orange, N.J., Jan. 2001.
Frand, J. L. "The Information Age Mindset: Changes in Students and Implica-
    tions for Higher Education." *EDUCAUSE Review*, Sept.–Oct. 2000,
    pp. 14–24.

Index